WAKE UP AND
SMELL THE POOP!

The myths, deceptions, lies and obsessions
that keep you from having the Perfect Dog®

By Don Sullivan
The DogFather®

Library of Congress Control Number:		2012904827
ISBN:	Hardcover	978-1-4691-8470-8
	Softcover	978-1-4691-8469-2
	Ebook	978-1-4691-8471-5

This book was printed in the United States of America.

To order additional copies of this book, contact:
Kaswit Corporation
1-888-574-5283
www.wakeupandsmellthepoop.com
Orders@kaswit.com

ABOUT THE AUTHOR

A former marine wildlife handler and professional dog trainer since 1986, Don Sullivan made his media debut in 2000 with his national Canadian TV show, *Doggin' It*. Wowing audiences with his seven-minute makeovers while working with dogs he'd never met before, Don went on to become a worldwide household name as the ultimate dog training expert, The DogFather®.

Sullivan hit the world stage in 2008 with his globally televised *Secrets to Training the Perfect Dog*® system. He's renowned for achieving amazing behavioral transformations in even the most extreme "bad" dog behavior cases, with positive changes seen in just minutes! Now in his no-holds-barred book *Wake Up and Smell the Poop!*, The DogFather® speaks candidly about the problems plaguing today's dog-crazed world.

For more information about Don's dog training system, "Secrets to Training the Perfect Dog®" visit www.theperfectdog.com.

MESSAGE FROM THE AUTHOR

I would like to begin by thanking the ultimate contributor to this book who granted me all my wisdom and understanding, the God of the Holy Bible and the Lord Jesus Christ—who also blessed me with many supportive, caring, and talented people to bring my knowledge and skills to a greater audience.

In particular, I'd like to thank Enrique and Angelica Molina who (apart from my wife) first believed in me and provided me and my family a strong platform of provision while I sought to expand my dream. Enrique and Angelica, you both went out on a very big limb, and to this day, I'm still in awe of the hand of support you offered us.

To Denise DuBarry Hay I offer my sincere gratitude for being the one to open the door of opportunity to me. Denise, you gave me the exciting chance to work with you—not as a client, but as a team member and friend. I will always remember your acts of graciousness toward me and my family. Plus, we had lots of laughs along the way, which is always a big bonus!

Most importantly, I would like to thank my beloved wife, Kaye, and ever-adoring sons, Ethan and Caleb. Kaye, you've been an encouragement to me from the day we first met, and your belief in me has never wavered. Ethan and Caleb, you have been a joy to my heart, and you've both joined in on the journey with eagerness and patience. Boys, remember how you each "took one for the team." Thank you!

Many thanks to my editor, Leslie Charles, and featured cartoonist, Leigh Rubin. Both of your contributions have certainly helped make this book something special.

To all my avid supporters, I thank *you* for giving me the chance to help transform your lives and that of your canine companions. Your success is a true delight to me, and I hope for a life filled with fun times and fond memories for you all.

If any of my readers would like to learn more about me and my family and our beliefs, I welcome them to visit the "About Don" page on my website: www.DogFather®.tv.

Sincerely,
Don Sullivan

PRAISE FOR THE DOGFATHER'S
PERFECT DOG® SYSTEM

Since my "Secrets to Training the Perfect Dog®" system was launched in 2008, hundreds of thousands of systems have sold all over the world, and my team and I have been overwhelmed by the number of positive emails we've received from delighted customers. The passion with which they've written their messages has been truly moving. It's been simply impossible for me to personally respond to every email, so I'd like to take this opportunity to thank everyone for sharing such amazing testimonies. The following is just a small sample of the variety of success stories sent to us. I hope you find them as inspirational as I have.

- Don Sullivan, *"The DogFather®"*

I received the DVDs and equipment Saturday morning. By Saturday afternoon before lunch, my Lab no longer pulled on the leash, was staying in the "down" position until called, and was able to beautifully retrieve (something she has struggled with since birth). Your program is easy and most of all, IT WORKS!!! Now I'm waiting for the next weekend to come because I'll be introducing how to handle distractions. Thanks, Don. *Justin M. Mesa, Arizona.*

I was home when I saw your advertisement on TV. I was skeptical at first, but with the thirty-day money-back guarantee, I told myself I had nothing to lose. We have a fifteen-month-old aggressive, hyperactive, and stubborn (but gorgeous) Yorkshire terrier.

I received the program two days ago. I immediately started with the training, and I'm so pleased with the result. My Yorkie has transformed into a totally submissive, well-behaved dog in a matter of days. Our whole family is enjoying him so much more. He is so well behaved that I thought something was wrong with him. We're no longer hesitant about letting him move freely around small kids and other dogs. We can now trust him, and we can tell that he is so much happier as well. Thank you so much. *Jeannette C. Livermore, California.*

First, I would like to say THANK YOU! Your system rocks! I have tried many types of training for my two Labs, and nothing has worked until I started with the *Perfect Dog*® system. I was shocked and amazed that you weren't lying when you said there would be a difference in only five minutes. I couldn't believe it, but now I certainly do. Thank you so much for this system. My five-year-old son can finally play in the yard without me having to lock the dogs in their crates. *Gwendolyn*

I am a dog trainer, and I absolutely LOVE your system! I've been working with dogs all my life, including clicker and positive reinforcement training, and these methods worked somewhat—but not to the degree that your techniques do! I've watched your DVDs maybe a hundred times now, and every time, the information sinks in even more. It makes so much sense!

I didn't actually have a reason for buying this system. I just saw it on TV and, being the person I am, curiosity got the best of me. I have six dogs: one was very dog aggressive on leash, three of them I couldn't trust to not run off after wildlife, and I could not trust any of them to walk by my side without a leash.

I can now call them back to me and they will all come, and I can walk the six of them through town without holding on to their leashes. Even the aggressive dog will now completely ignore barking dogs nearby! I'm very happy with this system. I recommend your system to everyone I can! *Amy H. Idaho, USA.*

After working with your program for just a couple of weeks, I have realized the difference is not only in how my dog behaves, but the way I feel about him. He's no longer just a pet; he is now a member of the family. Rather than leaving him at home because it's just too much of a pain to take him, he gets to come with us pretty much everywhere. I used to dread our nightly walks with him (I'd be so exhausted from him pulling on the leash the whole time), but now he heels without even being on the leash.

Even my family was amazed today. They have been in Europe for the past month and didn't know that I had purchased your training system. Every time they came over before their trip, my dog would jump up on them, and he was just a terror. They came over today and got here a bit early. We were not home yet, so they just let themselves in. As soon as we got home, we were asked if the dog was sick or if something was wrong with him since he was no longer jumping all over them and being a complete pain. They were almost dumbfounded to find out that simple training had made such a huge and positive change in him. Thanks, Don. *David C. Lincoln, California.*

My girlfriend has a Maltese named Teddy. He is five months old, and I thought that he was either stubborn or retarded because he refused to cooperate. When her dad sent her your *Perfect Dog*® DVDs and kit, I thought, "Oh boy, some hippie is going to tell me about dog psychology and compromises with dogs, etc." I was wrong. After watching the first DVD, I have seen marked improvements in Teddy's behavior in only two days! I don't care what anyone else says, YOUR PROGRAM IS AWESOME! That Command Collar® is also amazing. You truly are The DogFather®! *Daniel. Atlanta, Georgia.*

For more information about Don's dog training system, "Secrets to Training the Perfect Dog®" visit www.theperfectdog.com.

TABLE OF CONTENTS

FOREWORD

THERE ARE PEOPLE who come and go in our lives—some pass by with no more than a blink while others have a lasting influence. Sometimes it's because of what these people do, other times it's because of who they are, and once in a while, it's because of both. This was the case for me with Don Sullivan.

I've been in the infomercial business for two decades, and during that time, I've worked with a lot of people, some of whom have had great products and some not so great. In 2005, after selling the lion's share of the stock in my company and serving my contractual stay, I was ready to leave the business and go on to the next chapter of my life.

Having been an actress *(Being There, Black Sheep Squadron* TV series, plus appearances on *Charlie's Angels, Chips,* and *Love Boat),* entrepreneur (Malibu Yoga, Thane International, Blue Moxie Entertainment, Kaswit) and Coachella Valley celeb, my daughter—actress Samantha Lockwood— and I were featured in a local magazine cover story. Apparently Don saw the article, and he decided to contact me so we could discuss infomercial possibilities. By chance, he ran into my daughter Sam at the grocery store and told her, "I want to talk to your mother about marketing my dog training system."

When Samantha told me about Don's request, my immediate response was no. I didn't want to get involved with another infomercial; I wanted to do something different with my life such as getting involved in local nonprofit work or maybe producing a feature film. But Don asked if I would please check out his website before I made my final decision. That was the watershed moment for me.

When I saw the video clip demonstrating how Don Sullivan could train a very badly behaved dog in literally minutes, I was transfixed and overtaken with emotion. All the conflict and pain of having to give up my dog Brodie came rushing back.

Brodie was a beautiful, smart Border collie. An adorable puppy, he was my baby, but he had aggression issues we couldn't resolve. By the time he was eighteen months old, Brodie had attacked two of my friends. I had tried everything from Petsmart puppy schooling, clicker training and treat-based classes, to agility training—but nothing worked.

Thousands of dollars later, my beloved dog could climb ladders and do tricks, but he was still so randomly aggressive that keeping him had become too much of a liability. Giving up my dog was torturous. I cried and had bad dreams for weeks after relinquishing him to a training center that promised to find him a good farm home. Feeling like a failure, it seemed as if I was abandoning my child, but my dear Brodie was too much for me to handle.

After watching Don work with dogs, I knew I had to get involved. In our first meeting, I asked if he could have done something about Brodie's aggressiveness, and Don said, "Absolutely." With my heartbreaking experience still fresh, I knew it was my responsibility to get this training system out into the world. I knew I could help save dogs that might otherwise be sent to the pound (or worse). I knew I could help owners have a loving, safe, and rewarding relationship with their dogs.

I've now worked with Don for several years and have videotaped him working with at least fifty different dogs of nearly all breeds, sizes, and ages. The results are always the same. Dogs change so quickly in Don's hands that the astonished owners seem to forget their pets were ever badly behaved. Now that hundreds of thousands of *Perfect Dog*® DVDs have been sold around the world, I'm absolutely convinced that Don Sullivan's system has saved thousands of dogs from being destroyed.

Don's methods work so well that I dared to have a pet once again. I now have a dog that Don showed me how to train from the time she was eight weeks old. Pepper, my little teacup poodle, walks off-leash, always comes when I call, and she poops and pees on command. Pepper knows to stay on the sidewalk or grass, and she never ventures into the street when we take walks.

People are amazed at her level of obedience, and I feel secure and happy for Pepper that not only will she be safe, she has the freedom of roaming and sniffing that leashed or chained dogs will never have. After understanding and applying Don's methods, for the first time in my life I am an empowered dog owner, fully prepared to take on the responsibility of keeping a dog in my home—and my heart.

I feel very fortunate to have met Don Sullivan and know in my heart of hearts that he can help desperate dog owners from having to experience the pain and anguish I had to endure with Brodie. Don Sullivan is far more than a client to me. Don gave me the opportunity to represent a talented and wise man that can provide ongoing peace of mind and enduring enjoyment to dog owners and their pets. Who could ask for more?

Denise DuBarry Hay
La Quinta, California, USA

INTRODUCTION

If you allow for the possibilities of something better,
you move toward it instinctively. —Michael J. Fox

BARKERS. BITERS. CHEWERS and chasers. Runaways and rubbish rustlers. Growlers, gropers, jumpers, humpers, nippers, and crotch nuzzlers— I've seen it all. Maybe you have too. Chances are you have suffered the indignation, intimidation, or personal invasion of someone else's disobedient dog. Or maybe you've even owned one. Well, here's the message I'd love to bellow from the highest mountain peak: "It DOESN'T have to be this way!" *There is a remedy for every dog's misbehavior, and there is hope for every exasperated owner who's tried it all.* That's why I wrote this book.

Wake Up and Smell the Poop! is not a standard "how-to" manual, nor is it the rehash of trendy theories in the field of dog training. Rather, I answer some very simple, but deeply pertinent, questions you may well have asked yourself many times. For example, have you ever wondered why so many dog owners today are saddled with out-of-control canines while the world is flooded with so-called dog training experts, paraphernalia, and information? And despite the bounty of dog biscuits and drawers bursting with devices and gadgets, more dog owners than ever are desperately trying to create some semblance of peace and order within their homes. If you've ever wondered how such paradoxes can exist, stick around. You'll find out all of this and more.

Something is clearly afoul in the world of dog ownership and training. It's not that certain dogs are impossible to train (this is incredibly rare), or that the secret to having a well-behaved dog is shrouded in mystery and only accessible to a chosen few souls gifted with *the special touch*. It's nothing like that. The answers to training the perfect dog are plain and simple, but a multitude of contemporary training philosophies have systematically corrupted the average dog owner's perception of their animal's true nature, leading them seriously astray.

Many of today's dog owners are encouraged to endow their animals with human characteristics rather than try to understand and work with their pets' canine instincts. These people have been lured into embracing certain training styles because the methods appeal to human emotion. Some supposed animal experts exacerbate this situation by suggesting that canines have evolved to the point where they now bond more closely with human owners than their own species because they've lost their instinctive canine connection.

And let us not forget the scores of self-proclaimed animal whisperers and psychics who purport to read dogs' minds, hinting that mystical intervention is necessary to identify and fulfill a dog's true needs. But it doesn't end there; unfortunately and outrageously, the endless list of philosophical approaches, theories, and intervention tactics are overwhelming to say the least.

Do you smell anything? If not, I suggest that you inhale—in the deepest metaphorical sense, of course. Modern society is saturated with elaborate and enticing ideas on dog training that are presented as intellectually sound concepts, but instead are akin to the dreaded substance that needs to be scraped and scrupulously cleaned off your shoe after a misstep in a dog park.

Review the myriad of extravagant ideas and fanciful myths presented as fact in the world of dogs today and you might ask yourself how anyone could even *think up* such twaddle, let alone present it as a serious proposition. I'd consider it laugh-out-loud funny if it weren't so potentially disastrous, but thousands of gullible owners are buying into this madness. If, for example, it were indeed the case that your dog was becoming more "human," then you might want to be on your guard. Your precious pet could be itching to steal your car keys and take a spin around the block, rearrange the furniture while you're at work, or put *you* in a training cage for safekeeping!

As a professional dog trainer, if I could be granted one wish, it would be to travel through time with struggling dog owners where we could reverse the years of chaos and destruction, heartache, and disillusionment. I'd wish to help those frustrated folks create a completely different relationship with their dogs—a functional one and a perfect one. The methods exist. The route is there, to be sure, but it's too often sabotaged by the Western world's mentality of glorifying "all things dog."

Dog Daze

Considering the new definition of "family" dog, it's no wonder that in lieu of a logical, systematic approach to training, many owners try to coax or even guilt trip their dogs into obedient, socially acceptable behaviors instead of insisting on them. The intent may be admirable, but these owners act as if *reasoning* with their dogs will eliminate those pesky, unproductive misdeeds. I say dream on! This is an unrealistic and potentially perilous position to take, and there are many examples of such folly in this book.

There are people—more than you might think—who just adapt and try to live with the situation, no matter how intolerable it may be. This is an unnecessary and unreasonable option. Suffice to say, an owner's rejection of logic in favor of emotional projection or outright capitulation has all kinds of drawbacks, from slight to serious, and I cover this sad situation in great detail.

The most pathetic sight I've never been able to shake involved an elderly man driving his beat-up Ford station wagon with his head encased in a pair of industrial-strength earmuffs. Maybe you can envision the huge hearing-protection device protruding like boulders on each side of his head. The man's facial expression was nonchalant as he cruised along the road while his orangutan of a dog barked hysterically while hurling itself all over the car seats and against the windows, from the rear to the front and back again. I heard the shaggy beast's ear-splitting bellows long before the vehicle came into view.

I'm sure this ruckus lasted for the entire trip—in fact, for *every* trip this sad pair ever took. To me, this scene was one of pure insanity. It sadly represents the resignation of many modern-day dog owners who lament, "That's just the way it is." Maybe this story reminds you of a longsuffering dog owner you know; someone who needs to read this book. We all know at least one. Chances are, at some point in your life, you've been inconvenienced or irritated by a dog behaving badly and you wished "enlightenment" on the owner of the miscreant mutt. Sigh. Haven't we all!

The Dream Duo

If you're floundering in the turmoil of trying to train your dog, or you know someone who is, that frustrating lack of success could well be due to the influence of ineffective humanistic training philosophies. Other contributing factors might include media images and iconic portrayals promoting the impression that some dogs, unlike people, are simply born perfect; it's just a matter of winning the canine lotto. You either pull the winner—or you don't.

Hey, what dog lover hasn't daydreamed about owning a wonder dog like Lassie, the über dog of all time? Oh, to have that quintessential relationship, to stroll side by side down the dusty road of life, you and your ever-vigilant companion so aware of your every thought and emotion! Oh, to tackle every challenge or adventure together with quiet confidence and endless capability, regardless of the circumstance. Not leash, nor command, nor momentary mischief would ever ruin your rapport as the two of you travel through life in perfect harmony, on your way to ending each and every day on a blissfully happy note.

What a soul-satisfying vision this is. Yet for most people, a barrage of misbehaviors bulldozes this dream and blows it to bits within days, or even hours, of a new dog's homecoming. At first, the misdemeanors are tolerated or dismissed with a wave of the hand and a casual "Oh, that's just a puppy for you. He'll soon grow out of it." But alas, in time, the Lassie dream is replaced with a life tainted by leash pulling, permanent baby gates, poop smears and pee stains, demolished sofas, shredded slippers, and more, plus daily nagging at the kids to "Walk the stupid dog!" Some owners suffer a darker fate, with their dreams turning into nightmares. It doesn't have to be this way.

The Dream—Unleashed

Some dreams can come true, and the best ones take place in a context of reality. My *Perfect Dog*® training methods have been the answer for all kinds of people with all kinds of dogs. May I humbly state that I have helped thousands of dog owners around the world achieve a Lassie-type relationship with their dogs, and I want beleaguered owners who have "tried it all" to know that they too can enjoy the same results. Your dog may not have been born with a temperament perfectly suited to your human lifestyle (and I have yet to discover a dog that has), but with vision and persistence, you can help your pet quickly learn to perfectly adapt.

In my nearly thirty years as a professional trainer, my biggest joy has come from watching my clients rendered joyfully speechless as they see their dogs rapidly transform into obedient, ideal companions. One of my missions in life is to help dog owners create a satisfying, fulfilling, and lasting relationship with their pets instead of suffering endless stress and frustration. Not only *can* it be this way, this is how it should be—for every dog and for every owner.

People call me "The DogFather®," and in this book I unleash the secrets of how you too can have the perfect dog. I tell some hard truths, I don't pull any punches, and some of what I say is considered controversial. But if you can handle the ride, you'll be encouraged and energized by my ideas, stories, and no-nonsense approach to dog training. We'll even have some fun along the way!

CHAPTER 1

What you don't know can sometimes be exactly
what you need to succeed. —Don Sullivan

RUBES ®   **By Leigh Rubin**

"OK, fellas, we can hold up on the barking ... it's
about time for the neighborhood to wake up."

The Breakthrough

MOST DOG OWNERS make some pretty predictable errors in training
their pets. Maybe you'd admit to making a few mistakes yourself along
the way. I do. When you read about my childhood experiences with dogs,
you'll see that I certainly had my moments. Hey, we all have.

1

The all-too-frequent mistakes made by those of us who are all too human stem from a bundle of flawed assumptions and perceptions we pick up from family, friends, and people who think they have the answers. Our media-driven world is filled with myths, stereotypical thinking, and erroneous notions about "the way things are." When you stop and consider all the tips and techniques other people are only too happy to blithely pass along, you might marvel at the profusion of platitudes that abound. It seems that misinformation and misconceptions about how to train a dog are bandied about by many but only questioned or challenged by a few.

One of the most critical and confusing issues about training dogs involves the age at which a puppy's learning should begin. Should you start immediately? Is there a magic age of consent for dogs? Is it a mistake to begin too early or a bigger mistake if you start too late? These are some of the questions asked by caring or curious minds, and this marks the perfect spot for us to begin our shared mission of raising and creating the perfect dog.

When a stray puppy wandered into my life back in 1985, this pathetic little pooch was vomiting garbage it had consumed because it was starving on the streets. The pup was a German shorthaired pointer, perhaps twelve weeks old, and I felt compelled to adopt this needy little creature to save her from certain death. The friend I was staying with at the time said I could keep the dog, but only if I made the effort to properly train her.

Later that day, I visited the library and browsed the books on dog training. I checked out two volumes, returned home, and began eagerly thumbing through both books, looking for some clear direction on how to achieve the best and fastest results. But right from the start, it was difficult to understand what the books were attempting to explain. There were static photos with long, confusing depictions supposedly portraying what was happening in each image, but even after rereading the descriptions several times, it was impossible to decipher each exact training technique or how to properly apply it.

When I began reading, I had only felt ignorant. Now I felt both ignorant and perplexed—not the outcome I was hoping for! This library trip hadn't been the slam dunk I'd expected. Almost immediately, I realized the books contradicted each other about specific training methods. Each book emphasized a different approach, which exacerbated my confusion over *exactly* how to start my new puppy's schooling.

There was one important point of agreement between both books, however, and that had to do with the age at which a dog's training should begin. That I saw the same statement in each book clearly stands out in my memory: "A dog *must be six months old* before it can begin any serious training." The experts had spoken, and both authors agreed on this pivotal point, so I accepted their shared opinions as absolute fact.

Despite this single flash of enlightenment, I returned both books to the library a few hours later, overwhelmed from trying to understand and internalize so many conflicting ideas and approaches. So much for trying to educate myself! I ended up deciding that while waiting for my dog to reach that critical six months of age so we could start our "serious" training, I'd just try a few things with her that seemed to make sense to me. Who would have thought this was the best possible decision I could have made?

My Common Sense Made Sense

Doing what made sense to me turned out to serve us both remarkably well. To my surprise, I had my puppy "off-leash" trained within three weeks. This means that my dog was able to safely and obediently accompany me wherever we went—without a leash and collar. I could even confidently leave my puppy alone on the front porch of our house, which stood only a few feet away from the sidewalk.

Only once in the beginning of our training did she wander off the porch to follow a mother and her two small children as they strolled by. But after one correction, my puppy never stepped off that porch again unless I gave permission. She would come back from playing with other dogs when I called her, and she would lie down and stay without breaking the command, regardless of nearby distractions. I eventually named my dog "Wise"—not because I regarded her as an exceptionally brilliant animal, but because I believe God had somehow given me a gift of wisdom, a special insight and understanding into the nature of canines.

Recalling my early years of growing up with our family shepherd, I can attest that as a child I never demonstrated any particular talent for training dogs. But having achieved such resounding success with Wise, it seemed I was now blessed with an innate capacity for achieving remarkable results. This caused me to lose faith in what the dog experts had to say, and other than the two books I perused and promptly returned to the library, I have not read, nor have I referred to any other volume on schooling dogs. My current base of knowledge and proficiency in training canines has been purely God directed and self-taught.

As my expertise increased, I became acutely aware of the many behavioral issues dog owners were struggling with, and I decided to enter the world of dog training as a profession. After launching my new career, I found myself drawn to working with the more challenging situations. In due time, I became known for my ability to tame aggressive dogs, including ones that other trainers had given up on or refused to work with. And I repeatedly proved that puppies as young as nine weeks old could be trained to a level of off-leash obedience.

It Pays to Think Outside the Box

In doggie circles there was, and still is, the commonly held belief that puppies have very short attention spans, hence the fallacy that "puppies cannot focus, so you should not expect too much from them." Trainers would typically suggest, when working with a puppy, to only keep at it for five minutes at a time because the pup simply cannot concentrate any longer than that.

You might be interested in knowing that this common misunderstanding started with "experts" who assumed a puppy's mind is comparable to that of a human baby. Instead of trying to test or disprove this idea, someone at the forefront of professional dog training had proposed this narrow-minded notion, and it became generally accepted as a fact. The minute you hear the words "they say," I encourage you to consider whatever follows very cautiously.

Since childhood, I have always been one to ask questions and take issue with generally accepted ideas. I like to ask why, how come, and why not. This hasn't always made me popular, but it's certainly made me effective. Let's face it; many people are perfectly content to follow the masses, to embrace socially accepted notions without ever wondering if indeed they are true or not.

As kids, we are advised to go with the flow and "not to make waves." As a result, too many of us carry old adages into adulthood, where instead of inquiring or investigating, we perpetuate social myths and false impressions about how the world works. You might ask yourself what you once accepted lock, stock, and barrel until you found out it wasn't true. In this book, I will ask you to suspend some beliefs you might have about what it takes to train your dog to perfection so you can expand your horizons and achieve your goals.

Benjamin Franklin, Isaac Newton, and Albert Einstein did not become the brilliant men they were by passively accepting the thoughts of others—but by questioning, challenging, and thinking outside the box. All forms of today's accredited studies began with inquiring minds that overflowed with questions and challenges. As you know, scientific advances are the result of breakthrough discoveries made by those who put existing ideas to the test by asking why, why not, or how. Take any college course and chances are your studies will include a compilation of independent thinkers who were willing to investigate, discover, and devise new ideas, theories, or methods. Thanks to the courage and groundbreaking ideas of such astute minds, we enjoy many modern comforts and conveniences in our lives.

I've been privileged to formulate a number of profound, unique concepts in the field of dog training by engaging in my own studies instead of faithfully following accepted practices and philosophies. Thanks to my repeated experimentation and discoveries, I enjoyed success early on in my efforts to learn how dogs learn. In other words, rather than pursuing a traditional education in animal behavior, I charted my own course. And it worked. In this book, I offer you and your dog a breakthrough experience that will greatly enhance your relationship and the quality of your lives.

The World Is My Classroom

In 2005 I was the keynote speaker at a conference for veterinary assistants. Some of the attendees were already working in the industry while others were students finishing their degrees. I was asked to speak about handling aggressive dogs in the workplace. The night before my speech, my family and I visited the campus to check out the facilities and test the equipment for my PowerPoint presentation.

Stepping out of our car, we noticed a cluster of eight young women strolling along the sidewalk. Each of them was being led by a large dog, and I couldn't help but notice that each dog wore a head halter device. Although I'll never forget this scene, what happened next made me regret that we human beings don't have video cameras implanted in our foreheads.

On the other side of the street, a man was walking his dog. As soon as the eight constrained dogs noticed the interloper, bedlam ensued. The dogs began barking and baying, hauling on their leashes, literally dragging some of the women into the street to get at the unsuspecting dog. The chaos continued until the lone dog and its owner disappeared around the corner.

My curiosity piqued, I initiated a conversation with one of the dog walkers. She told me they were all students in the veterinary assistant program (the very audience I would address in the morning), and knowing I had seen the chaos, she mentioned that animal behavior and handling were part of their studies. She praised the program, proudly emphasizing that all of their training methods were positive and that corrective discipline was never used.

When I was introduced on stage the following day, I'm sure the eight young women were surprised to see me because I hadn't revealed my identity at the time. My introducer was the head of the animal behavior program, and as I began my speech, I wondered if she might later regret having invited me once she heard some of my ideas on proper dog training.

We Are Accountable

Thanks to my insights from the canine horror movie I had witnessed the night before, I made some radical adaptations to my presentation. Instead of speaking on how to handle dogs in the workplace, I covered the critical issue of *accountability*. I urged my audience to understand that their clients regarded them as experts in "all things dog" and that they were partially responsible for the aggressive traits exhibited by dogs that were brought to them. I then cited the example of the farcical dog handling I had witnessed the previous day and how dangerous it could have been if any of the dogs had broken free.

I spoke with passion about the need for discipline in dog training and denounced their vehement opposition to its use in correcting undesirable or aggressive behaviors. I stated that an altruistic or idyllic attitude without behavioral limits or boundaries seriously undermines the objective of creating a well-trained animal, while the application of discipline could have brought every one of those eight unruly beasts into line within a matter of seconds.

At the end of my two hours, I appreciated the department head's diplomacy as she politely thanked me for my presentation; it must have been very difficult for her. I walked away hoping I had persuaded someone in that room to question current methods, to think outside the box and use common sense and logic instead of conforming to generally accepted assumptions.

Maybe, just maybe, someone truly heard my message about the

importance of *discipline* in training because every person in that room was accountable. And, as dog owners, we are accountable for what our dogs become. For both dogs and owners, the subject goes far beyond mere quality of life. Consider for a moment the issue of potential life and death—I am not exaggerating. We are all accountable. You already accept that fact, or you wouldn't be reading this book.

CHAPTER 2

Regret for things we did can be tempered by time. Regret for things we did not do is inconsolable. —Sydney J. Harris

Removing the Rose-Colored Glasses

PEOPLE CAN'T HELP but be enchanted by the impressive grace and harmony as they watch the choreography between marine mammals and trainers at theme parks. Swept away by the magical—often flawless—performances, you can safely bet that some dog owners are sitting there, transposing those visions of teamwork to their own situations with their dogs at home. Human nature being what it is, people want to believe that if this apparent oneness can be achieved between human beings and powerful giants such as orcas (killer whales), then surely, training a dog to such perfection should be a walk in the park.

During my stint as a part-time marine mammal trainer at Sealand in British Columbia, I worked with orcas, seals, and sea lions. In our performances, the other trainers and I would guide the creatures through their established routines to the delight of adults and children alike. It was an awesome experience, working so closely with these magnificent creatures that most people only dream of getting to see, if they're lucky. During breaks, I would go to the whale pool and lie down at the edge of the water. Soon, one of the whales would swim over and roll upside down, knowing I would obligingly rub its belly. To me, each of the whales seemed like big, wet, slippery dogs with fins, and it was a thrill being so close to them. I never took those special moments for granted.

Because of my credentials as an established dog trainer, I enjoyed the privilege of bringing my dog Wise to work each day. Most of the time, she would lie on her blanket under the counter in the room reserved for the park's trainers and animal care specialists, but I also got to take Wise out onto the viewing deck where she could roam freely with me. One of my favorite photos shows us strolling on the deck. My trusty dog is off leash at my side, and on my other side is Salty the sea lion. Seeing these two mismatched creatures ambling along as if it were the most natural thing in the world still brings back a feeling of joy. It was emotionally enriching to witness my dog sharing the fullness of my life, and we had this freedom because I could trust her to behave impeccably under such unusual circumstances.

Go Fish

I arrived at some critical conclusions during my employment at Sealand, and the lessons will stay with me for life. You may be aware that the core training principle for shaping the behavior of marine mammals often centers on food as a reward for desired performance, and this was the practice at Sealand. We fed fish to our oceanic "trainees" as a means of motivation and positive reinforcement.

Here's how it worked: we would sit with our seal pups, and when they engaged in simple, repeatable behaviors, we'd reward them with a piece of fish for their "performance." Some of the pups had quirky behaviors that were unique to them (head bobbing, slapping their fins, or opening their mouths as if to smile). We would link a specific word with each behavior and reward our subject with every successful completion of that movement. Eventually, we would incorporate these behaviors into an act that would become part of the show.

There's another term for positive reinforcement used by those who feel the need to make it sound notable and scientific. It's called *operant conditioning* and, having been intimately involved with this process, I prefer calling it "bribery." Yes, I admit that this approach got results, but only on a superficial level. In truth, we trainers were the ones being trained as we learned to recognize desired behaviors and immediately reward them. For our seabound stars, responding to food as a reward did not equate to obedience, only performance. And it certainly did not earn us trainers control over the creatures. Not at all.

Food for Thought

The proponents of "palatable payoff," or *food as reward*, suggest that it's an effective way to train a dog, but I adamantly disagree. There exist some potentially serious drawbacks to operant conditioning because this method has significant built-in limitations.

In our work at Sealand, there were times we trainers would step out on stage only to find that some of our mammalian cast members were not keen to work that particular day. The usual reason was that they had been overfed during the last show, which made them unmotivated by the bucket of fish we used to coax them. Our only solution was to momentarily ignore the offending culprit and then warn the next show's trainers about the refusals so they wouldn't use that animal until he was hungry enough to cooperate again. Other times, we found that some of our slippery stars were simply feeling mischievous, and they would choose to give us a hard time.

In the marine show, we didn't consider it a big deal if one of the creatures was unwilling to perform. Yes, we trainers would look a little foolish when we said, "Now, Salty here is going to ring the bell for us!" and she would simply sit there with a blank stare, as if *we* were the ones who were supposed to perform the trick! It was embarrassing, of course, but there was no imminent danger. Either the performance went off without a hitch, or it didn't—and the audiences were remarkably forgiving. In fact, so were we, the Sealand trainers. We simply tolerated those moments; what else were we supposed to do?

The Doggone Truth

Let us always keep in mind that canines are vastly different from marine mammals. For one thing, your dog lives by your side 24/7. You are always accountable from a personal and legal stance for your dog's "performance." For that reason alone, I can state without question that responsible dog training needs to involve *consequences*. My point is that if you attempt to achieve obedience from your dog by solely using food as a reward, you risk creating potentially dangerous outcomes for both of you.

Consider for a moment that if your dog has been trained to come *only* because it wants something from you, what happens if your pet decides there's something more fun or interesting going on? What recourse do you have when your dog chooses to run away instead of toward you when you call? Maybe you'd agree that the most common owner's strategy seems to be yelling the dog's name repeatedly with ever-increasing volume, despite the fact that it isn't working. We've all witnessed this one.

Let's take this scenario up a notch: if there's a road that lies between your dog and whatever it's hotly pursuing, the results can be disastrous. Many of us have heard the tragic story of an out-of-control pet that met its end under the wheels of a speeding car. But it's not just runaway pets. Consider the number of unprovoked dog attacks where innocent people or other dogs are injured, and you get the sense that food training simply isn't enough. Such needless losses don't have to happen, and this is why I emphasize the need for discipline and not *just* reward in dog training.

One dog trainer, disturbed by the thought of using physical correction for dogs, phoned to berate me after viewing one of my TV appearances. In an accusing tone, she said, "You didn't use your disciplinary methods on the whales, did you?" No, we did not, and that was why our circus-trained animals were not always reliable. We were accustomed to those occasional refusals to perform, but little did anyone suspect that our "no consequences" training would result in a tragedy.

Trouble in Paradise

A problem developed at the theme park as one of our sea lions became increasingly aggressive. His name was Sailor, and he had become somewhat of a stalker. When we were on stage, Sailor would leave his station, sneak up behind us, and bite us on the backside. This wasn't just a playful nip, and more than once, a female trainer ended up in tears after a show because she had received a fairly severe bite.

Our troublesome sea lion was the son of a monster-sized fellow named Clyde. Clyde was a most amicable guy to work with, a very sociable and even huggable galoot. We all loved Clyde. But his son Sailor was becoming more and more bold, and nothing we did would curb his belligerence. While our head trainer held a degree in animal behavior, he might best be described as a new-age type. He was a proponent of operant conditioning, the style of training that had become all the rage.

Concern over Sailor's escalating acts of aggression began to grow. In my work as a dog trainer, I had successfully tamed numerous aggressive dogs out of their dominant tendencies, and I was seeing absolutely no improvement with Sailor using operant conditioning. I was aware that Sailor's father, the gentle and kind Clyde, had received a completely different type of training—and that's why Clyde was such a reliable guy. It was clear to me that Sailor's problem was worsening because the new head trainer's philosophy and methods lacked any kind of consequence for bad behavior.

I approached Sealand's general manager about the situation, offering to work with Sailor until his aggression issues were resolved. The manager liked my plan and agreed to let me do the work. But the head trainer intervened before I could begin working with Sailor, and the general manager reneged on his promise to let me help.

Here's how the head trainer's plan went: whenever Sailor stayed in the water and *didn't* sneak up to bite us, we had to reward him with a piece of fish. The core principle of this method was solely reward based; there was never to be any consequence or punishment for Sailor's aggression. But in the middle of the act, as we focused on our show duties, Sailor continued his aggressive moves, sneaking in a quick bite in the blink of an eye. It really galled us that he seemed to be thoroughly enjoying these naughty acts of rebellion.

From Bad to Worse

Sailor's attacks became more frequent and more brazen. Despite our pleas and protests, we trainers were becoming victims of this ineffective training strategy, stuck in a vicious do-nothing cycle that was spinning out of control. There's a saying that if you keep on doing the same thing you've always done, you'll keep on getting the same results. Well, our head trainer insisted that we continue his methods, despite the fact that his system wasn't working. If you think this sounds insane, we thought so too.

Things now went from bad to worse. We began having problems with one of the killer whales: Tilikum (often misspelled Tillikum). There was a moment in the show where we would invite a member of the audience to come down to the stage, where our special guest was given the opportunity to rub a whale's tongue—a sensation the whales seemed to enjoy. You can imagine what a spectacular moment this was for the audience that an everyday person got to *touch* a whale! It was a novel experience we all enjoyed.

However, Tilikum had begun closing his mouth and then quickly opening it whenever his tongue was touched. We trainers sensed that he was merely playing a game, but before we were able to figure out how to correct this quirk, things fell apart. One day, an elderly woman was selected from the audience to pet the whale. Not only was it obvious that she was a senior citizen, she was also blind. No doubt, she was chosen with the best of all intentions, perhaps to add a touch of pathos and drama to the show.

I was in the bawckroom when I heard a commotion over the PA system. Tilikum had closed his mouth on the lady's hand but did not immediately open it as he had always done before. The twenty-two-foot-long whale almost pulled the terrified woman into the pool before finally letting go. Imagine the alarm and embarrassment on the part of park management, not to mention the horror stories that would be told by the stunned spectators. From that day on, audience members were no longer allowed to participate in our show.

A Very Unhappy Ending

Between the head trainer's inability to correct the escalating behavior problems and the general manager's do-nothing attitude about these ineffective practices, I was completely exasperated. After tolerating this no-win situation for several months, I quit my job at Sealand in disgust. Once again, I went back to my dog training career full time while feeling sorry for my frustrated trainer friends who felt trapped in their jobs because they had nothing else to fall back on.

The tragedy took place some months later when the female trainer who replaced me accidentally fell into the whale pool with Tilikum and two females, Haida II and Nootka IV. The three whales immediately blocked the young woman from any possible escape. One of them grabbed and dragged her to the bottom of the pool, where they played with her as if she were a rag doll. The game continued for some time, with the whales surfacing and tossing the trainer back and forth in the air, and then hauling her beneath the water again and again. Meanwhile, the topside trainers did everything they could to call off the whales. They blew whistles and slapped buckets on the water—the sign to come for a food reward—hoping to distract the whales and regain control, but none of their frantic efforts worked.

The whales deliberately ignored every attempt to get their attention or interrupt their play. This was the first time a human being had been in their pool, and the orcas were making the most of it. The whales had no idea they were killing the girl; there was no way the mammals understood that she couldn't breathe underwater like them. But they were having a new kind of fun, and there was no stopping them.

Just like that, a human life was lost. I was sick at heart when I found out what had happened and, at the same time, grateful I wasn't there to witness this disaster. The victim, Keltie Byrne, was only twenty years old. A court inquest followed this catastrophe, and as a former employee, I was called to testify. Shortly after the court proceeding, the decision was made to close Sealand down for good. The whales and other creatures were shipped off to new locations where their careers as marine performers continued.

Playing with Lives

On February 24, 2010, Tilikum struck again, and this time it was no accident. You see, the giant orca went from Sealand to Sea World in Orlando, Florida—where his history was expunged and he became a big star. Near the end of his popular Dine with Shamu show, audience members watched in horror as the six-ton monster deliberately seized an unsuspecting veteran trainer in his jaws, hauling her beneath the water to her death.

At forty years of age, Dawn Brancheau was one of the park's most experienced trainers. But in the blink of an eye, she became a helpless victim to this beast's murderous intentions. Terrorized bystanders in the underground viewing area witnessed the whale swimming by, flipping the bleeding victim around in his mouth.

Brancheau's death was one more addition to the string of violent incidents involving killer whales at marine theme parks around the world. Since the 1970s, over two dozen people have been injured by orcas in captivity, and a handful of these attacks have been fatal.

The most insidious part of this grim scenario is the lack of acknowledgment that these mammals are actually wild and unpredictable, and denial occurs even when signs of danger are evident. At the time of Brancheau's death, marine park visitors reported that earlier in the day, the whales had appeared unsettled and were being unresponsive to the trainers. But for park management, the adage "the show must go on" prevailed.

In 2006 when a trainer at Sea World, San Diego, was nearly drowned by an aggressive orca, I contacted the *NBC Today Show* affiliate in Los Angeles to comment on the incident. I told them about Keltie Byrne's death at Sealand, hoping this would instigate some policy changes that would prevent another whale trainer from being killed. Although the Sea World whale had deliberately seized the trainer's foot in his jaw and held him underwater for over one minute, reports on the San Diego incident grossly downplayed any element of danger. Knowing how Keltie had died, I felt compelled to dispute such denial and dismissal.

I was taken aback to learn that no part of my interview with the LA station was aired. Instead, the reporter primarily focused on showing some feel-good footage of him swimming with Sea World whales a year earlier. I contacted another TV news channel, hoping they would expose what seemed to be a PR cover-up—after all, theme parks are big business, and big mammals draw big crowds. But once again, I was stonewalled. Either no one felt my information was important or valid, or a lucrative enterprise was using its influence to stifle outrage and sway public opinion in its direction.

The 2006 attack took place four years before Dawn Brancheau met her fate in the giant Tilikum's jaws. These incidents involved different marine park locations and different orcas but shared the same set of circumstances. Human beings were using mere fish in an attempt to control the behavior of potentially dangerous creatures, with no responsible parties willing to openly accept or admit to the reality of the risks involved.

The trainers were, in effect, playing with their own lives. And those who were in a position to put a lid on this risky game allowed it to continue as if nothing could or would go wrong, despite past incidents to the contrary. I'm horrified to think they still are.

The Potential Is There

These needless, appalling attacks and deaths serve to reinforce the insight I gained early on at Sealand. With any potentially dangerous creature that shares an intimate relationship with human beings (dogs included), it is essential and critical to include *accountability, discipline,* and *consequences* in a training program. If this is not possible, then the parties who are in charge need to question the practice of continuing creature-human interactions when lives may be at stake.

You see, for show whales there are no consequences for disobedience; there are only rewards for desired behaviors. Carefully consider this gaping void, the complete and utter lack of consequences in the current whale training programs, and it's no wonder these marine giants totally disregard their trainers under unique or unusual circumstances. In the absence of consequences, why shouldn't they?

We've been discussing marine mammals, and now let's bring this home lest the point be lost. Your dog is a domesticated animal, capable of far more than you might think—good or bad. You share a special relationship with your pet. But even so, as a dog owner, you never want to take anything for granted. Those rose-colored glasses through which you sometimes view your dog need to be replaced with some lenses containing shades of reality. You want to clearly envision and work toward satisfying outcomes for all concerned—your dog, your family and friends, and yourself—where safety, unwavering obedience, and respect for boundaries are of prime importance. That's where real training comes in. And that's what this book is all about.

CHAPTER 3

There's a world of difference between a dog that is off the leash and a dog that is trained to be off the leash. —Don Sullivan

Rubes®   By Leigh Rubin

Fetters or Freedom?

ONE OF MY clients told me a bizarre story about a dog he had once owned. Cruising full speed ahead on a desert highway, his two-year-old springer spaniel sat beside him in the passenger seat. It was a lovely evening, and both car windows were down. Suddenly and amazingly, a bird flew in the passenger window and out the driver's side. Before the fellow could blink, he caught a flash of his dog leaping across his lap and out of the car in hot pursuit of the bird.

My client slammed on the brake, eyes glued to the rearview mirror as his beloved companion disappeared into the dusk. By the time he stopped and turned his car around, it was difficult to figure out exactly where the mishap occurred. Fearing the worst, he walked along the middle of the road, waving his flashlight from one side to the other. To make this story even more outlandish, the man finally found his terrorized dog in a shallow gully alongside the road, in shock and shaking profusely, sprawled atop the body of a road-killed deer! The happy news is that the springer made a full recovery, but he was forever banned from riding in cars with the windows down.

Restraining Order

When I talk to people about off-leash training for a dog, I'm often met with the argument that all dog owners have to restrain their dogs because leash laws must be obeyed, and therefore, off-leash training is rendered useless. Many contend that they would never dream of taking their dogs off leash anyway because it could be unsafe. Yet the springer spaniel story is a perfect demonstration of why I promote off-leash training. Unexpected things happen, and when they do, the dog's life could be at stake. If my client's spaniel had been trained to ignore distractions and self-monitor (the happy result of training your pet to behave responsibly when he is free of a leash or other restraint), the dog would never have vaulted out of the moving car.

Off-leash capability means far more than a dog roaming about freely and eventually wandering back to its owner when it feels like doing so. People can take their dog to a park and let it loose, contending that the dog has a natural need to run and explore. In fact, this is done all the time in the hope no one will notice or object. Owners often assume that because their dog eventually comes back after a few calls or coaxes, this means their pet is "fairly" well trained. And hey, if it happens to chase a squirrel or get into some small mischief while loose, this is pretty much par for the course; after all, a dog is—well, a dog. In my mind, this is a pretty low performance bar. These people who corrupt the idea of off-leash training may as well distribute leaflets with disclaimers apologizing in advance for any obnoxious behaviors their dogs might engage in while "running free."

Certainly, the use of a leash may prevent certain doggie misbehaviors, but that's not my point. We're talking about the role of *training* in dog ownership, not the use of physical restraint. I believe all dogs have the right and the ability to exist in our human world without having to be restricted by leashes and collars. I also believe all people have the right to be protected from bad (and potentially dangerous) dog behavior. But despite my beliefs and convictions about this issue, I recognize that off-leash freedom can only become common practice when, as a society, we all begin to fully understand what a well-trained dog is capable of. Right now, we're a long way from that ideal.

I yearn to see the day when off-leash training is an everyday reality among dog owners, but it won't happen on a grand scale until we realize how our human nature unconsciously works against this radical change. Here's what I mean: many people might *see* the need for change and even protest or talk about the subject (add any global issue here; it doesn't just have to be about training dogs), but that doesn't mean it'll happen. Change requires unlearning (letting go of what we think we know) and relearning (embracing a new way of thinking and behaving), and this is difficult.

In the beginning of any social movement, those individuals who actually achieve personal transformations are the exception, not the rule. But they can be catalysts of change for their peers, family, friends, and more. In time, their influence can be immense. Your very act of reading this book and applying the principles within can result in your making a huge contribution toward liberating dogs and their owners from the many societal myths and misrepresentations that dominate our thinking. You can help eliminate the dysfunctional, restrictive belief system that prevents owners from fully realizing their dog's incredible potential.

Concealed Chains

If you saw a person inflicting cruelty upon a dog, you (and any other passersby) would instantly come to the rescue, and we can hope it will always be that way. Yet have you ever considered that there is a subtle, socially acceptable form of abuse toward dogs that occurs in private and in the public eye every day? No one stops it. Few question it. Only a select few notice it exists at all.

Let me introduce you to what I regard as some everyday forms of canine incarceration. The most common act of imprisonment is that of constantly confining dogs to a three-foot shackle, otherwise known as the leash. Then there are the dog pens, baby gates, or the family pet being relegated to the laundry room or a cage when guests arrive. Just to twist the knife a little deeper, let's add banishment to a commercial kennel at vacation time because the dog just isn't well behaved enough to take on long trips. This is merely a sampling of the second-class citizen treatment some people give their pets without blinking an eye.

Dogs in these situations watch the world slip by from the periphery, never having the opportunity to fully participate in the wonders around them because they haven't been trained to the point where they can be fully trusted. These dogs' lives would be entirely different if only their owners would raise their bar of expectation and wholly embrace what I know to be a realistic and reachable goal.

Imagine taking your kids to a playground and then forcing them to hold on to your hand while they watch other children playing on swings and slides, running around freely and enjoying their adventures. How long do you suppose your kids would stand at your side before they begged you to let go so they could join in on the fun? Imagine saying something like, "I'm sorry, kids. You have to stay here with me. I love you so much I don't want you to hurt yourself. If I let you go, you might run away or get injured because I've never taught you how to stay safe." You might further explain you're happy to bring the kids to the playground every day so they can watch the fun, but only on the condition that they stay connected to you.

It goes without saying that, despite your good intentions, you'd be inflicting pure mental and physical torture on your kids. Any kind soul witnessing this fiasco would label you as twisted, mean, or possibly abusive. At the absolute least, you'd be considered irresponsible for failing to educate your children in social skills and safe conduct. I contend that this analogy is parallel to what millions of dogs around the world are forced to endure every day of their lives.

From Captive to Captivating

A year after my favorite dog Wise died, one of the cameramen from my Canadian show told me about a dog at the pound I might be interested in. He said that she might be put down soon because of aggression issues, so I rushed over to take a look. She was indeed aggressive; in fact, she bit the shelter employee who was conducting the dog's adoptability analysis. Not a good move! But the dog was a Weimaraner-Labrador cross, and she possessed the body style and size I was looking for, so I took her home on the spot, confident I could work out the behavioral issues.

For the first three days, Esther threatened everyone who came near my property, and even those who looked like they might be thinking about it! I laughingly tell people that I could have offered anyone a thousand bucks at this stage, and no one would have ventured into the pen with her. Whenever I entered her space to feed her, Esther would attempt to bite me. But she soon came to realize that I wouldn't tolerate her reign of terror, and she began to simmer down, quietly watching my clients and their dogs as they came and went. Within ten days, I had her fully off-leash trained.

At this same time, my dad fell ill and was hospitalized. I flew to see him, taking Esther with me. I walked into the hospital and up to the third floor with her heeling beside me, minus a leash or collar. We entered my dad's room, and I told Esther to lie on the floor and stay while I made a quick trip downstairs. When I returned to the room, three hospital staff members were standing there, raving about the obedient dog that didn't move a muscle the entire time I was gone. Esther had now been with me for less than two weeks.

Air Apparent

Esther enjoyed a privileged life, and I don't mean she was spoiled in any sense. She enjoyed a lot of freedom, and she earned it. When I flew from San Francisco to Seattle for a TV appearance on ABC's *Northwest Afternoons* program, Esther was granted permission to fly in the passenger section with me. Not only was this a special honor, given that she was a large dog, it was the first time such an exemption had been granted to a nonservice dog.

If you are wondering how it was that Esther was allowed such privileges, here's what you would have seen if you'd been with us: *I'm walking through the airport with a large, lean, shiny black dog that is heeling perfectly by my side. She is without leash or collar. We arrive at the security check-in where I remove my shoes, belt, laptop, and so on, while my dog, calm and alert, stands beside me. I point, which tells Esther she can now walk through the metal detector. She goes through and turns to face me, positioning herself next to the security guard on the other side. I follow, gather my things, and put myself back together. Esther continues to watch me, and when I signal we're ready to head out, we proceed toward our gate, side by side.*

From outbound to return trip, everywhere we walk in both airports, we're greeted with smiles and stares. Esther and I are allowed to preboard the planes and are treated like royalty because it's such a novelty to see a big dog behaving so perfectly in public. The entire trip was a delight. It was a deliciously rewarding experience because it was such a wonderful demonstration of what a dog is capable of in the real world.

A Dog's Life

Esther was not a "superdog," nor was she an exceptionally responsive creature. She was simply trained using a system that tapped into her full potential. She had earned her freedom. It was always her choice to unwaveringly submit to my "alpha" authority, and because of this, Esther was truly part of our family, accompanying us on many exciting adventures. She never had to be excluded because she was never a bother or risk. Now *that*'s a dog's life! Esther was a perfect example of a life liberated from potential oppression and even destruction. In no time at all, her required confinement was replaced with the wealth of trust and freedom as my training methods revealed her true capabilities.

Judah, our current dog, is a German shorthaired pointer with a story similar to Esther's. I found Judah in a shelter for wayward juvenile canines. He was nine months old and had been incarcerated because of his aggressive tendencies. Judah had apparently developed a liking for chickens—meaning he had already killed a number of them. My first impression of this dog was that he was quite high-strung and very self-absorbed. You could equate his behavior with that of a hyperactive child who has trouble focusing. This turbocharged dog seemed to be bouncing off the walls within his own mind.

Judah had interesting markings, but he didn't seem particularly handsome to me; maybe his wild personality overshadowed his physical attributes. During the two-hour drive home, he seemed to settle down, but when we finally stopped to let him out, we realized why he had become so quiet in transit. Our new dog had vomited all over his travel kennel. We had just adopted Queasy Rider.

Getting Our Feet Wet

We didn't take our new dog home right away. Our first stop was a public park where there lived a resident flock of ducks. After washing our new companion's lunch off his coat, I placed a training collar around his neck and we headed for the duck pond. I wanted to set the record straight, that I would not tolerate any aggression toward other living creatures. I figured ducks were as close to chickens as I could get, and I hoped they'd do the trick.

As soon as we approached the closest duck, Judah lunged. To his surprise, he was sternly corrected for his transgression. I now had his attention! As we approached more ducks, he was slightly wary but ready to test how consistent I might be in my discouragement. Judah found yet again that I was *very* serious about him ignoring these birds. Now many people—including some in the dog industry—would argue that the dog was "only following his instincts" by going after feathered friends. This is true, but it didn't mean he was incapable of controlling his natural desires. He was now learning that a whole new behavior was being required of him. After only two corrections, Judah walked around the duck ponds much more calmly, acting as if he and flocks of waterfowl had been peacefully coexisting for years.

We took Judah home, introduced him to his new environment, and got him settled in for the night. The next morning, I allowed him to socialize with a stray miniature poodle that was staying with us until it could be rehoused. This was a dog we had found wandering in the middle of a road one week earlier with no identification. I should add that the poodle was a cocky little male wrapped in a deceptively fluffy exterior.

Initially, the two dogs seemed to be okay with each other, but a few minutes later, I heard a commotion going on in the backyard. Judah was attacking the poodle. I was impressed to see the smaller dog holding his own against a much larger dog, but this altercation was unacceptable. I shouted and charged into the fray, pulling Judah off the poodle, once again delivering a correction that conveyed my deep displeasure with his aggressiveness. Judah had a crazed look in his eyes when I first got hold of him, but moments later, he looked very humbled.

Seven Days Makes One Meek

Over the next few days, I took Judah to as many places as I could think of where circumstances might tempt him to act out. Even the *indicator* of aggressive behavior earned him a correction (he must have thought I'd gone psychic on him), and he was quick to figure out what was expected of him.

A week after adopting Judah, I was asked to appear on a TV show to discuss and demonstrate effective dog training. Judah, now off-leash obedient, and I made our entrance. Unbothered by the cameras, lights, and studio audience, my dog quietly walked on stage, dropped down at my feet, and proceeded to wow the audience. It was both educational and entertaining for people to see Judah's calm demeanor while listening to the story of how aggressive he had been only seven days earlier.

Toward the end of my interview, a five-month-old exuberant black Labrador puppy was brought on stage and handed over to the host. This was to be my "challenge" dog for demonstration purposes. Despite its leash, the Lab yipped repeatedly, jumped on the host, and scurried in circles, behaving like the perfect poster child for an untrained, highly excitable puppy. All this time, Judah lay on the floor in front of me, still obeying the "down" command I had given him when we first walked on stage.

My challenge, as the show's dog training expert, was to be given only seven minutes of working backstage with the pup to see what could be accomplished. Another guest would be interviewed on camera while I did my thing, and then the puppy and I would return for our demo. This show was filmed "live to tape"—which means the cameras never stopped rolling, so my seven minutes with the puppy was to be exactly that and no more. There were two things I planned to accomplish. First, I would teach the pup not to pull on the leash (the beginning steps of my off-leash training program) and second, I would teach him a "down, stay" command.

The Great Unveiling

When my seven minutes was up, we were called back to the set. I was reintroduced and asked to show the audience what, if any, improvements I had made with my hyperactive charge. Despite the live studio audience, the bright lights, the large cameras moving in and out, and the host standing near us to welcome me back, the pup walked calmly beside me on a loose leash.

Before sitting down, I pointed to the floor and told the pup, "Down." He dropped to his belly on the first command. I said, "Stay," dropped his leash, and then took my seat. The pup lay there with a slightly regal air, almost as if to say, "No big deal. I've always had my act together like this." Needless to say, everyone in the building was dumbfounded. The puppy held its position, still obeying my first command, even as the host reached over to give it an approving pat. The very same pup that had wildly jumped all over the host just a few minutes earlier was now on the floor beside me, not breaking his command, despite the many distractions in the studio.

One of the beautiful things about this transformation is that not one piece of food was used to bribe this puppy. Many myths were shattered that day in the minds of the people who witnessed this transformation. The pup's potential had been revealed in a matter of minutes. People mobbed me after the show, telling me how stunned they were at what they had seen.

For Judah, the show was, in a way, similar to opening day at an international auto exhibition where the new, exciting vehicles are suddenly unveiled for the waiting crowd. This was Judah's unveiling. In only one week, he had become a different dog; he was a new creature, ready to discover what adventures lay ahead for him now that he could be trusted.

Do Not Try This at Home

To illustrate the extent to which you can train a dog, here's a remarkable example. However, I must first issue a "consumer warning." What you're about to read would be considered by many as irresponsible and reckless, especially by those who work in the dog industry. Those who consider themselves to be all-knowing will adamantly assert that no matter how much training a dog has had, a dog is still an animal that is, at times, incapable of controlling its natural-born instincts. These "experts" would state that a dog can't ever be trusted one hundred percent. From my experience, I believe otherwise.

Please bear in mind that I *do not* recommend that you or anyone else try the following stunt. It was something I knew without question that my dogs could handle, and I built it into their skill set as a demonstration of the degree to which dogs can comprehend and respect road safety.

While living in British Columbia, at times I would drop my dogs off on a randomly selected sidewalk in the community. I would then proceed to drive, following the flow of traffic, while my dogs ran along the walkway, off leash, keeping pace with my vehicle, never once venturing into the road. Whenever the dogs reached a cross street, they would slow down and look to me for direction. I had taught them to always stop at a street corner and never cross unless invited. As my dogs would approach the intersection, I would call out "wait" if the light was red and they needed to stop. They would then halt at the curb until my next instruction. If the light was green and it was safe for them to go, I would yell "okay," and they would then proceed to cross the street, continuing to shadow my vehicle.

Just to allay any possible concerns you might have, I must emphasize that my dogs were incredibly fit. They had also developed unwavering confidence in my leadership, and I trusted them implicitly. This was in no way an exhausting or distressing exercise for them. On the contrary, whenever I would let my dogs out of the vehicle to begin this routine, their bodies would quiver with such delight that they looked as though they were dancing, excitement bubbling through them like a child entering Disneyland for the very first time.

On the Road

You might be interested in knowing that for my dogs, the command to stop before entering a roadway was so ingrained that it even proved effective in unusual environments. There were times when my dogs and I would be hiking in the mountains and they would wander ahead of me on the trail. They might go around a bend and out of sight while staying within what I considered our established acceptable roaming range. Sometimes, as I'd make my way around a switchback or trail loop, my two dogs would be standing there, halted at the edge of a dirt service road, patiently waiting for me to catch up. I'm convinced they had the ability to discern that the width of the road meant it was a passageway for vehicles, so they knew it was out of bounds to cross without permission.

Over the years, all of my dogs have viewed our backcountry outings and city adventures as just one more part of their exciting lives. Yet if I had allowed certain societal pressures to contaminate my vision, such as believing that canines are incapable of such high levels of obedience, my dogs and I would have never been able to experience such thrilling accomplishments.

I approach most things in life with the mind-set of exploring the limits and pushing the boundaries to maximize the chances of achieving what I believe is possible. I like to get a feel for what the limits *truly* are to ensure that I don't allow assumptions, fears, or predisposed ideas to sabotage the fullness of a prospective outcome.

Because I have chosen to live my life with a "maybe I can" vision instead of wearing "I can't" blinders, I've opened up my world to all kinds of outcomes others might have deemed impossible. Not only have I benefited immensely from this perspective, so have my dogs. I hope this encourages you to reflect on the so-called impossibilities you've already achieved in your life, and the ones you still want to tackle, especially with your canine companion. Never underestimate the power of vision.

CHAPTER 4

How sure we are that everyone's watching.
How sure we are that no one sees. —James Richardson

Rubes®   By Leigh Rubin

Officer Johnson runs into
one of those "gray areas" of the law.

Get Your Dog on a Leash!

AS I BEGIN this chapter, the words "Get your dog on a leash!" are resounding in my ears. We have just returned from a family bike ride during which we were rudely and unjustly berated for having Judah, our dog, off leash. This is not the first time I've been yelled at or even verbally abused about unleashed dogs, nor will it be the last.

29

This unfair situation exists for two reasons: First, it's impossible for observers to discern that my dogs are behaving as if they *are* on a leash. People simply can't comprehend it. Second, most people have marginally trained dogs that *must* be leashed, so when these individuals are presented with owners like me whose dogs have impeccable manners, we end up being labeled as lawbreakers. Go figure! If logic prevailed, it would be the other way around. But then I'm getting ahead of myself.

My dogs are trained to roam within a specific radius where they are free to run and explore without disrupting anyone's personal space or property. This self-governance provides the dogs with intense exercise and maximum enjoyment of their outings. At the first sign of other people or their pets, my dogs are trained to return to a heel position until the passersby are gone. This is something I enforce out of respect for others. Of course, when my dogs are given an invitation to interact, I allow them to "go see."

Perception Is Not Reality

The bicycle trail we rode today is in a residential area. There are homes on either side of the bike path, some of which are fairly close to passersby. Judah was, as usual, abiding by our rules as he ran along the trail about ten feet in front of us. As we approached a home on the bend, there was a commotion on the deck. I looked up to see a well-dressed man holding the collar of his large yellow Labrador in an effort to restrain the dog as our family pedaled by.

My immediate thought was that the man seemed to be having some kind of disciplinary issue with his dog, and as we slowed to a stop, Judah halted with us and looked at the scene on the deck. Without a word or signal from any of us, Judah held his place on the trail, watching and waiting. The man glared at us and angrily yelled, "Get your dog on a leash!"

I was quite shocked by the man's outrage and tried to reassure him that my dog wouldn't come anywhere near his place. But despite the presence of my young children, he swore at us, saying, "I don't give a bleep! Get your dog on a leash!" Knowing there was no way to reason with this man, I simply motioned for my family to move along the trail, and we went on, shaking our heads at what had just occurred.

To analyze this event from both perspectives, on the one hand you have a man with a large, out-of-control dog he is attempting to hold back so it doesn't bolt and cause trouble. On the other, you have a happy, nonintrusive dog quietly standing close to his family, giving absolutely no indication that he will leave their sides and invade the man's private world. So I ask you, what's the problem? Or better yet, *who* is the problem?

The Blame Game

I struggle to understand the confused logic that prompted this man to panic. He and many others like him are the victims of irrational thinking. Here's what I mean: the guy's dog is obviously misbehaving, but the man gets mad at an innocent bystander. So do you suppose that my having Judah on a leash would have motivated the guy's dog to be more obedient? I've accomplished a lot with my training methods but, somehow, have never managed to perform anything *that* miraculous!

I'm sure you grasp the unrealistic expectations that lead to these types of outbursts. Even when *leashed* dogs walk by, that man's dog will still go nuts. It's not a leash issue; it's that no one has trained that yellow Lab to exhibit any kind of self-control. And as long as the owner keeps blaming everyone else when things go wrong, he'll never do anything about his dog's delinquency. The Lab wanted to get at my dog simply because Judah was there.

What happens to the dog on the deck when children go by? If the kids are tossing a ball back and forth, and the Lab wants to grab it, would the owner swear at the kids or their parents, or the ball? Would he demand that they quit playing with the ball because it's bothering his dog? The sad possibilities are endless, and you may be wondering what might happen when squirrels or bunnies run along that path. Negligent, ignorant dog owners make it hard for the rest of us.

Certainly, if a dog can't be trusted off leash, it's the owner's responsibility to keep the dog in tow. The man with the Lab evaluated us from his position of suffering the antics of an untrained dog; he couldn't grasp that any owner could have the kind of control we have with Judah. He incorrectly assumed that all dogs are the same, that all dogs would behave like his dog if it ran free.

It's indeed an indictment of our societal "groupthink" mentality that the majority of dogs are held to such low standards, and it's unfortunate that so many owners suffer the frustration of ineffective, insufficient training methods. Because of this shortsightedness, when the average person observes a dog so well trained it seems to possess almost humanlike abilities, it is impossible for them to fathom.

The Ties That Bind

Some people might argue that leashes are a precautionary measure, providing a sense of safety for others that a dog will not infringe upon their personal space. But is it fair to impose a blanket leash law on *all* dogs? Are leashes truly a social or legal necessity?

The state of modern-day leash laws is very much a Catch-22 situation. These laws were created to control bad dog behavior in public. Yet, as I state earlier in this book, canine misbehavior primarily exists because of popular positive reinforcement bribery methods, embraced by owners and dog industry professionals alike. As long as inadequate training continues, owners will never be able to attain the level of off-leash responsibility I know is possible. Training dogs to the level of self-governance as I've done with mine (and those of my clients) could persuade government officials to evaluate and reverse rigid, restrictive leash laws.

Under current circumstances, all dogs and owners are considered "guilty as charged" without a chance to prove their capabilities, but radical changes could take place if we eliminated the real perpetrator—ineffective training! If we as a society focused less on leash laws and more on results-based training that teaches a dog to self-govern and behave responsibly when off leash and under intense distraction, dogs and their owners could enjoy the freedom and enjoyment of the outdoors they deserve. No longer would we be barraged with badly behaved dogs. The now frequent complaints about unprovoked aggression and reports of attacks to the authorities would significantly diminish, and officials would be more open to allowing the public to self-manage. The government could establish required behavioral standards for dogs to be granted off-leash freedom while irresponsible owners that breech those standards could be fined. This way, the proper parties, those in violation of the law, would be punished instead of the innocent.

We are undoubtedly a long way from my vision of general acceptance that dogs are capable of acting in a mature and responsible manner without being constantly confined to a leash in public. Yet we have to begin somewhere. If we don't change our perception of the possibilities that lie within our reach, dogs and their owners will never gain the freedom they yearn for and are entitled to. The number of family dogs around the world continues to increase year after year, but unless the current inadequate training trend is curbed, the future quality of life for pets and their owners appears dismal. I hope we will one day reach a time when self-governing dogs and their responsible owners are allowed to enjoy their lives to the fullest, and the impulsive, discriminatory knee-jerk command of "Get your dog on a leash!" will go the way of the dodo bird.

CHAPTER 5

If you think education is expensive, try ignorance. —Abraham Lincoln

Creators Syndicate, Inc.   rubes2@earthlink.net   5-1
© 2002 Leigh Rubin!   www.creators.com

"OK, boy, let's try it again ... "

Ignorance Is Not Bliss

CONTRARY TO COMMON belief, dog training is not a long, slow process that takes endless amounts of patience and will consume most of your free time. When consistently applying a logical, discipline-based, results-oriented method, you achieve useful and lasting results in far less time than you may think. But unfortunately, this approach seems to be the exception rather than the rule. Many people are swept away by the promises of popular gurus, current trends, and social pendulum swings that favor ineffective training methods. Consequently, many easily resolved problems go uncorrected or only partially addressed, resulting in headaches and heartaches down the road, further perpetuating the myth that training a dog can take years and sometimes even last the duration of a dog's life.

A distraught woman once phoned me because their family dog, a two-year-old golden retriever, had bolted out the door and into the street. The dog was hit and killed by a car right in front of the caller's two daughters. You can imagine the emotional toll this took on both children, especially the younger daughter who sought refuge in her home, refusing to attend school. She suffered from nightmares and clung to her mother's side to the extent that professional counseling was required. The woman called me because the family's second dog had the same problem of sneaking out the door and running around the neighborhood at every opportunity, and another pet loss would be devastating.

This tragic incident would never have happened if effective training methods had been used from the beginning. Thinking they were doing the right thing, the parents had allowed their eleven-year-old girl to enroll the golden in classes at the local community center where they used the food-based bribery approach I so despise. Things seemed to being going well at first; the daughter enjoyed her time bonding with the dog, and each lesson came wrapped in a warm and fuzzy style that appeals to youngsters. But it wasn't long before the dog became too much for her to handle on a walk. The parents were convinced that the dog was just going through a "teenage" phase, as others had suggested. But it was more than that. Way more. And the end result had been another sad story of a dead dog in the middle of a road.

My point is not about irresponsible dog owners. It's about irresponsible dog trainers and supposed experts teaching worthless methods that leave owners without the control they need for order and safety. It's about offering training that fails when unavoidable distractions or potentially dangerous circumstances occur. In this case (and many others), if the training had indeed been effective, a much-loved family pet would still be alive.

What We Don't Know *Can* Hurt Us

Simply put, the sad state of affairs in dog training today centers around ignorance. According to the *Webster Dictionary*, ignorance is: *(1) having little or no knowledge; unlearned. (2) unaware; uninformed.* The majority of those associated with today's dog world (trainers, groomers, veterinarians, rescue groups, pet store owners and employees, authors, and other self-appointed experts) have no clue that the type of training they promote can only achieve limited results. In fact, their methods often exacerbate certain problem behaviors instead of fixing them, and in my mind, this is ignorance at best and malpractice at worst.

For example, when a toddler munching on a cookie is slammed to the ground by a neighbor's food-obsessed dog, this child is a victim of the positive reinforcement "treat as reward" training movement so popular around the globe. Even more culpable are the trainers who recognize the shortcomings of their training methods, but succumb to social pressures that suggest discipline is mean and food is a form of kindness.

Here's the acid test: if dog owners are looking for, hiring, and working with multitudes of trainers all over the world, why are there so many misbehaving dogs? In every neighborhood, dog park, veterinary clinic, and grooming salon there are aggressive dogs, disobedient dogs, and naughty dogs. Yet the Yellow Pages, bookstores, pet stores, specialty magazines, Internet, and TV are saturated with dog training schools, advice, and contrivances.

As you can see, something is clearly wrong with this picture. There's a serious disconnect. The American public is spending millions of dollars on training its beloved canine pals every year, yet dogs seem to be getting more and more out of control. As the saying goes, we need to wake up and smell the roses—or in our case, the poop! We as dog owners need to summon our courage and be willing to initiate a canine cultural revolution.

Pride is the first cousin of ignorance, and because of human pride, experts in the dog industry refuse to admit that dogs are the big losers under current practices. Some owners, deeply enmeshed in justifying their emotional and financial investment, contribute to the facade by pretending that the training is working. While I am generally quick to help relieve struggling dog owners of guilt over their pet's misbehaviors (despite supposed proper training), my sympathy wanes when I'm faced with resistance, weak arguments, or blatant rationalization.

An Exercise in Frustration

In 2006, I spent a few months in Santa Barbara, California. I would visit the various city parks to let my kids play and allow our dog Esther to run. My sons, who were three and five at the time, often played a game with our dog that always impressed onlookers. Using an old racquetball racquet, my boys would hit a ball and wait for Esther to retrieve it. Whenever she brought the ball back, she would gently place it on the racquet, even when my three-year-old held it. If the ball happened to roll off the racquet due to human error, she would simply pick it up and try again.

One day, my older boy was enjoying the retrieving game with Esther. As I looked across the park, I saw a fellow with a young vizsla some distance from us. His dog was on one of those ridiculous but popular retractable leashes, and I wryly watched their comical, chaotic gyrations. Picture a deep-sea angler that has just snagged a huge fish and is being heaved about in a multitude of directions while becoming entangled in the line. Add an ample supply of raucous barking, and you can begin to appreciate the spectacle this pair presented to onlookers. The man attempted to regain his dog's focus by frantically waving a treat in front of the dog's nose.

I could restrain myself no longer and made my way over to the dynamic duo. As I approached, the dog lunged at me while the owner struggled to stop the rapidly extending leash. Before the man was able to secure the lock, the dog charged, jumping on me and leaving his signature paw print on the bottom of my clean shirt. Not only had the dog left his mark, he hit me with ample force in a most sensitive area.

After the man's obligatory apology and my politely restrained response, I introduced myself and offered him one of my business cards. He refused it, asking in a rather cold tone, "What type of *method* do you use?" He said he was currently working with a local trainer, asking if I had heard of the fellow in a tone implying that everyone knew this local legend. In fact, I had heard the name a couple of times, but only when I had approached other dog owners laboring to make their dogs behave.

I knew I risked offending this man's pride when I began to outline some of the obedience issues he was wrestling with. Like sprinkling salt into a freshly opened wound, I told him I could correct some of the dog's problems in minutes. But the insulted owner defaulted to that all-too-common position of resistance to new information. He had to justify his emotional and financial investment instead of considering that I might indeed be able to help him.

Apparently, he had been working with this "trainer of choice" for six months and was now eligible for free boarding at the trainer's kennel whenever he traveled. The man revealed he had spent over $3,000 on his dog's education so far, and the trainer had recently suggested that he just needed to spend more time working with his dog because it was "still just a puppy, after all."

We Look, But Do We See?

I directed the man's attention to where my sons were playing with our family dog. By now, a few other children had gathered, and they all took turns hitting the ball for Esther to fetch. I told the man about Esther's background, how I had found her in the pound and how she had been only days away from being destroyed because of aggression issues. I'm quite sure the man thought I was grossly exaggerating when I told him it only took me ten days to train her to the level he was witnessing.

Here was Esther, a dog running freely in a park without a leash or collar, playing with a bunch of little kids respectfully and with quiet enthusiasm. This man had been indoctrinated to believe that dog training is a long, slow process that requires endless measures of patience, time, and money—plus tolerating "puppy" mistakes instead of correcting them.

Yet again, here's that old saying: If you keep on doing the same things you've always done, you'll keep on getting the results you've always gotten. That so describes what I run into all the time! When I approach people about their bad-mannered mutts they get defensive instead of receptive. Resistance to contrary information is so drilled into their subconscious minds, they can't comprehend that there are other choices. To further complicate things, there's the issue of self-worth to consider.

A lot of owners simply can't admit that what they're doing isn't working. So many "invested" owners walk away from free help that could change their lives and that of their dogs, just to save face. My wife has been a steadfast sounding board and source of comfort as I try to understand the stubbornness I so often witness. People frequently turn away from me and march off into the distance after refusing to be shown a few simple things that could make such a difference in their lives. In effect, these individuals prefer to continue struggling and suffering along with their dogs to save their pride.

If the above evidence isn't enough, consider the excuses made by owners who have been bitten by their own dogs. Dog aggression is seriously misunderstood, and I have a lot of empathy for those who end up victimized by their own ignorance. But at the same time, I'm both astounded and alarmed by the number of people who reject my simple and clear explanation of what's behind aggressive behavior and how it can be treated. Instead of considering a new way of thinking and perceiving, many people dismiss all logic and cling to their mistaken notions, determined to continue on their wayward path.

Many people who suffer bites from their own dogs find it almost impossible to comprehend that their pets know *exactly* what they are doing. During auditions for my second TV infomercial, I spoke with the owner of a dog-aggressive Jack Russell/corgi mix. Whenever she took her testy pet to the dog park, he would challenge and threaten other dogs. She told me how one day, her dog instigated a very nasty fight. As she impulsively reached in to separate the two dogs, she found herself on the receiving end of her dog's aggression. He tore at her right breast, puncturing her skin and leaving her bleeding profusely. She was rushed to the emergency room.

Denial Is a Dismal Excuse

A lot of owners perceive that being bitten by their own dog while attempting to break up a fight is an accident, but that's not really what's going on. I counter that the fight—and the bite— didn't have to happen. There's more to the story of the woman who was so seriously injured by her dog. I had an opportunity to discuss the details of the incident with her, and I wish you could have seen her facial expression as she told me the following, with complete conviction: "That night, my dog and I were on the couch, sitting quietly. He looked up at me with such a remorseful look in his eyes, as if to say, 'I'm so sorry I bit you. I didn't mean it.'"

She was shocked when I rejected her assumption. I then explained that in her dog's mind, she had long ago established herself as his subordinate in "the pack" by failing to correct his aggressive tendencies. Consequently, when she got involved in his fight, he penalized her for stepping out of line. The dog deliberately used his teeth as a message to back off. He was clearly telling her that, as his follower, she had no business interfering with his leader business.

This misinformed woman so desperately wanted to believe that the bite was an accident, she refused to even consider that her intervention represented a challenge to her dog's authority. This is yet another example of owners imposing human motivation over canine instinct. This kind of mythical thinking perpetuates not just frustration but serious potential danger for an owner or innocent bystander.

You've Got to Believe it Before You Can See It

People often say that "seeing is believing"—but in the case of dog training, it's actually the other way around. You can't "see it" till you believe it. Many dog owners are stuck in this conundrum, but they need to accept that all biting incidents must be interpreted as acts of aggression. People are also flabbergasted when I categorize barking as an expression of canine aggression, yet it is.

Barking is generally a warning signal that dogs are prepared to escalate their aggression should the perceived threat continue. You can consider barking as the warning of a possible bite. Many dogs bark, and fewer bite, but that doesn't mean your barking dog would never bite. You can regard the barking dog that hasn't yet bitten anyone as a dog that has not yet been in a situation where it has felt the need to bite.

A lot of people say about their dog: "Oh, he's just all bark and no bite," or "Don't worry, my dog would never bite you." These naïve statements can put a stranger or visitor in potentially perilous situations. Take, for example, the household dog that barks at people on the other side of the door. This dog is, in effect, communicating to intruders: "This is my territory. I want you to clearly understand and accept that I'm the leader here, and should you challenge me in any way, I'm fully prepared to defend my dominion." In most situations, nothing happens because the visitor doesn't do anything that the dog views as a serious threat. But we mustn't kid ourselves; the potential is always there.

Because you are reading this book, I perceive that you are interested in learning about how dogs think, and I hope this will change the way you view a barking dog from now on. As you know, when confronted with a barking dog, most visitors typically enter the home with a bit of caution, gently offering an outstretched hand near the dog's nose, hoping for approval. Wise visitors keep their body posture subdued, avoiding any sudden moves, while speaking softly and soothingly. Faced with such a nonthreatening approach, the dog assumes the person got the message, so he "holsters" his gun.

If, however, a visitor were to boldly walk in, talking loudly and displaying emphatic gestures (as can often happen with excited children), a dog that has never before been challenged could possibly escalate to the next level of aggression. The owners might be shocked, wondering, "Where on earth did that come from?" Yet if the owners better understood their pet and how

41

it perceives the world, they would have noticed that the signs of aggression were always there.

These same principles also apply to how dogs interact with each other. If two dogs are barking at each other, they are figuring out which one of them owns the position of dominance (the alpha dog). Don't fall into the trap of foisting human characteristics on these animals; they are not saying "hello" to each other. My point is that their "conversation" is far more complicated and vastly different from what most owners or observers believe. Once you understand what's really going on, you will perceive dogs in a truly different light: a more realistic one.

Making the Message Meaningful

Many people operate under the assumption that a barking and growling dog means their pet is a good protector of hearth and home. As a result, these owners (and too often, their neighbors) put up with a lifetime of useless noise. They may suppose that one day this ruckus might come in handy in case someone breaks into the house, but really, how often does this happen? The reality is that when trespassers do intrude, very often the family guard dogs are found by the police, lying dead in a pool of their own blood.

Consider that if a dog is allowed to bark at family members, friends, the people next door, and falling leaves—how can owners ever differentiate everyday disturbances from real ones? A lot of owners don't realize that most dogs are incredibly intelligent, sensitive creatures, possessing the ability to discern between a nonthreatening, casual visitor and a hostile intruder with evil intent. Even though you might teach your dogs that barking and growling are unacceptable, which is what I have always done, your trusty pet will very likely warn you if a threat arises.

I say this based on experience. Some years ago, I had two dogs in my life: Wise, my German shorthaired, and Augie, a retriever/pointer cross. Working with my dogs from the position of accountability, discipline, and consequences, I banned all forms of barking from the get-go. I knew if I tolerated even the slightest woof, it would open the door to additional problems. For years, I never heard either of my dogs bark or growl. Any vocalization from either dog would simply be sounds of joy or pleasure during playtime romps and vigorous ear rubs.

But one afternoon I was at the beach, resting in my truck, parked as close to the ocean as I could get. Wise and Augie were dozing inside the fiberglass canopy in the back of the pickup. They were so quiet, no one would have guessed there were dogs inside my vehicle.

As I gazed at the sky and water, enjoying the approaching sunset, I began to hear growling. At first, I thought I was hearing someone else's dog in the vicinity, but then I realized that the sounds were coming from the back of my truck. I straightened up and checked the rearview mirror. Sure enough, I spied a suspicious-looking man who was trying to peek through one of the canopy windows, as if scoping it out for possible loot.

Many people, strangers included, had been that close to my vehicle before. Some had even looked inside while my dogs were in there, and all of these times, my dogs had remained completely unperturbed. In this case, however, I am convinced that Wise and Augie sensed something was wrong. Somehow, they knew this prowler was up to no good.

I believe dogs can sense evil intent, and they have the intelligence to correctly discern when growling or barking is warranted, but they have to be trained. Even dogs that have consistently obeyed the no-barking rule can instinctively know they need to alert us when danger is near. This is one of the many benefits of building a solid, respectful dog-owner relationship that is founded on obedience, responsibility, and mutual trust. This isn't make-believe or the Lassie syndrome. This is what's possible when owners respect their pets enough to provide them with proper training.

CHAPTER 6

"Assume nothing." —C. Michael Armstrong

Follow the Leader

MY TRAINING METHODS are based on a canine, rather than human, perspective—that is, my approach simulates how dogs function in a pack. Every canine group has a hierarchy, with an established leader and a pecking order of followers. Canines are gregarious by nature, and because each dog comes to know its place in the hierarchy, all pack members are free to enjoy the camaraderie of the group.

The leader of a dog pack is both respected and loved. All enjoy his presence, yet each follower is ever aware of the leader's dominion. This is because the leader at some point will discipline or dominate each and every member, earning his place of authority. In other words, the leader holds pack members accountable for their actions. When subordinates step out of line, they momentarily suffer the consequences, but this strictness produces respect, loyalty, and steadfast love for the leader.

Speaking the Language

Of course, we human beings can't discipline our dogs in the exact fashion as a pack leader would, but we can simulate canine language with techniques that gain our pet's attention and respect. For example, a firm "no" on your part equates to the throaty rumble, growl, or bark a mother dog will use to keep her pups in line. Just as a small child might choose to ignore a parent's injunction, puppies will sometimes tune out their mother's signals or outright disobey. When ignored or challenged by a willful offspring, the mother dog reinforces her message by regaining her pup's attention with a nip.

I designed my Command Collar® for this very purpose. My collar emulates the quick but effective nipping action that a mother dog uses to maintain order in her family. This means that if your dog chooses to ignore your verbal commands, you can physically reinforce your message. And just as the mother dog assesses what level of correction is necessary to obtain a satisfactory response, you can adjust the level of the collar's "nip" to suit the individual dog.

A lot of people make snap judgments about the use of my collar as a means of physical reinforcement, demonizing the method even though they have no understanding of the purpose or principle behind the device. Please stay with me through this entire discussion because there's a lot to be learned. You can find out what's right about the kind of training collar I invented and discover what's wrong with the traditional type of collar used every day by owners around the world.

Most people don't realize that the common flat nylon or leather collar only *restrains* rather than trains a dog. A flat collar should never be used on an untrained dog because it offers no serious behavioral consequence, and it can cause significant physical harm. The only purpose this type of collar should fulfill is to carry a dog's registration tags. This is because when an untrained dog pulls against the leash, the flat collar inflicts steady, intense pressure on the dog's throat instead of a quick disciplinary signal as a mother dog might impose.

While scores of dogs have acquired severe trachea problems from pulling against a flat collar, who objects to—or openly criticizes—this potentially harmful device? Thanks to social programming, a lot of owners think the flat collar is the only training tool they need. There are other pseudo training devices; perhaps you've reviewed the multitude of complex to flamboyant head halters and harnesses, but don't even give them a thought. They are as useless in the reinforcement of commands as would be a plaintive plea to "please don't do that."

Getting Attention, Gaining a Relationship

Now and then, when owners first see my Command Collar®, they are taken aback. When I catch the look on their faces, I explain that—like the swift action of a mother dog teaching her puppies to respect her commands—my collar works quickly, consistently, and effectively. In dog language, the message to pay attention and obey is expressed in a way that is easily and effectively understood. Once clients understand my collar's relationship to canine communication, their concerns are allayed and they are good to go.

The Command Collar® is for dog owners who want to maximize their pet's potential by establishing a cornerstone of obedience, freedom, and self-governance. It's not for fans of trendy training philosophies built around wonder gadgets or designer doggie treats, nor is it for people who are quick to judge and slow to modify their opinions. It helps to remember that many of the technological or medical advances that are now common practice were initially criticized or even demonized. And not too long ago, skeptics were questioning how the Internet could possibly hold any value for the average person.

Yes, there will always be detractors. And there will always be gurus who claim to have special powers or employ an esoteric hands-off training process. The real losers, of course, are the dogs that will end up leading lives of confusion and incarceration because they can't be trusted.

My collar is for people who want results, levelheaded owners who are willing to do what it takes in the short term to create a long-term life of mutually enjoyable companionship. Just as canine pack leaders or mother dogs take short-term action to establish order and harmony, once the rules are instituted and the hierarchy sorted out, the frequency of discipline diminishes to a maintenance level. At this point, the pack members are free to enjoy and enrich their relationships. Similarly, my Command Collar®, used in conjunction with my Freedom Training Lines and DVD instruction, is a temporary tool that opens the door to the highest levels of respect and freedom, and a fulfilling long-term relationship for both the dog and owner.

My clients continually state how richly satisfying it is to suddenly realize that your now self-governing dog no longer needs any training equipment because the two of you have reached the "trust zone." Just as your dog wholly trusts in your leadership, you can trust your canine pal to freely operate within the accepted boundaries. But achieving this level of connection is not solely dependent on the use of my training equipment. You are a critical component in this venture, and the first and most important step is your ability to retrain your human mind toward "dog think."

A Dog's World

When people acquire a dog, they consider it a member of their family, but the dog sees things differently. Clueless about the canine mind-set, few owners grasp that the human environment in which dogs exist represents "pack life" from their pet's point of view. From the moment its feet touch down in a new home, a dog (regardless of its age) immediately begins assessing each person in its family as either a leader or a follower. If the dog perceives a lack of leadership in the new pack, he takes on that role until the time he might be challenged for the position.

No matter which role the dog assumes, whether leader or follower, he will always want to love the other pack members. This is where many owners become undone because they assume that a dog's love or devotion (call it what you will) equals instant submission to the owner's authority. In the animal kingdom, submission to the leader is essential for preservation, order, and harmony. In pack context, the word *submission* simply means "holding to the natural order." Because the leader is responsible for, and interested in, maintaining each subordinate's well-being and survival, it's his job to establish and preserve control. It's the same for you when, as a loving and responsible dog owner, you motivate your dog to submit to (or accept) your leadership for the purpose of his safety, health, and satisfaction.

When Bad Assumptions Happen to Good People

Most owners make two big mistakes in how they perceive the relationship they share with their dog. Both of these misconceptions are based on wildly erroneous assumptions that beg for enlightenment. First of all, the owners assume that their dogs *must* absolutely, with no question, hold them in high regard because the owner is (supposedly) the higher life form. The mentality goes like this: *I bought you, I own you. I am the human being, and you are the canine. Therefore, I am superior.* The dog, of course, is thinking no such thing.

The second mistake involves the owner assuming that he or she is the dominant one solely because of the difference in size. This is especially true for owners of smaller breeds. Little dogs have to literally look up to their owners, but from the dog's point of view, this has nothing to do with respecting the owner's authority. People unconsciously project all kinds of emotional inferences on their dogs—for example, perceiving that their poor helpless munchkins are defenseless, completely dependent creatures that need protection and patronage. It is unfathomable for many owners to even for a moment consider that their dog might actually be the one "wearing the pants."

We are describing two different worlds between owners and their dogs: two remarkably different sets of assumptions and perceptions existing between two strong-minded creatures with incredible potential. The most regrettable part of this culture clash is that very few trainers ever enlighten (or are *able* to enlighten) owners about how dogs think. And only a tiny percentage of owners ever figure this out on their own. Given all this, it's no wonder so many dogs misbehave. Every now and then, I almost want to bang my head against the wall because this gap can be so easily bridged with proper education. That's my mission, and I hope this book makes a difference.

Owners of small dogs and puppies are easily duped into softening their training approach because of their dog's appearance. Many owners freely admit they are pathetically lenient because their "darling dog" is so tiny and defenseless. They confess that if they owned a large, powerful dog, they would be more assertive or consistent. This is not a mere human foible to dismiss or smile at; this is a glaring perceptual error with the potential for woeful consequences. *People don't realize that their dogs perceive leniency as subordinate behavior, not as a favor or an act of kindness.* Consider the implications of these two disparate viewpoints. This is just one more example of owners attributing human characteristics to their pets instead of attempting to understand the relationship from a canine point of view.

Unintended Consequences

In the 1950s, a brand-new superhighway system was built across the United States with the intent of connecting people from one end of the country to another, but it had the opposite effect. Instead, people became more mobile, spreading out and moving away from their hometowns in droves. This was an unintended consequence that no one had predicted. Well, unintended consequences happen to dog owners too. Consider how often you witness an owner protectively whisking her little fluff ball into her arms as a large dog approaches from up the street. Her intent is admirable (she wants to protect her beloved baby from the jaws of a potentially big bad beast), but the owner has no clue she is creating unintended consequences. She is actually encouraging aggression in her own dog by communicating fear.

In her dog's mind, those shielding behaviors on the owner's part establish her as a submissive pack member. The little prince, perceiving his pack member's apprehension, will attempt to defend her; and he'll drive the threat away by barking, snarling, and struggling to free himself from those overly protective arms so he can do his job.

The owner believes that her dog's outburst is an expression of fear, not an attempt at dominance, and her angst increases because her little lovely is clearly distressed. The dog, sensing the escalation of anxiety within his subordinate, remains on guard until the peril has passed. As the big bad dog and owner disappear, the little dog rejoices in yet another victory in protecting his pack from a threat. Both the owner and her dog have played off each other's emotions, and the owner is completely oblivious as to who was actually protecting whom.

Let me state once again that if we want to maximize our training success, we need to adjust our methods to match the way a dog's mind works. We have to quit assuming that dogs are "furry four-footed people." If this owner could analyze the situation from the standpoint of pack dynamics, chances are she would give up those protective behaviors that create such an undesirable outcome. Were she instead to assume a firm position of leadership, she would have a secure, peaceful, and calm dog that defers to her in all situations. She would feel more confident about her role as an owner and her dog's ability to self-govern. And here's the best part: if the owner were to alter only that one "shielding" reaction to perceived threats when she and her dog are in public, she would most likely witness improvements in other areas of her dog's behavior patterns too.

Just to be clear, I'm not suggesting that you should never protect yourself or your dog from obvious danger, but there are subtle ways of handling certain situations without jeopardizing your leadership position. For example, you can cross to the other side of the street well in advance of nearing a potential aggressor, or turn a corner and go a bit out of your way to avoid a nasty confrontation. But strategic avoidance should *only* be used in extreme circumstances, or your dog will never learn how to effectively deal with his surroundings.

Good Training Transfers Above and Beyond

I often tell my clients not to be surprised if, following the first training session, they begin noticing that certain problem behaviors (ones that have not yet been directly addressed) suddenly disappear. It's rewarding to discover that, as soon as you begin working with your dog in a manner that logically reflects his way of thinking and perceiving, you will earn his respect. Even better, your dog will start transferring your training to other parts of his life.

Without your having to specifically address them, mischievous behaviors such as incessant barking, begging, or outright food thievery may disappear. This is because you have begun to effectively enforce new boundaries in your relationship, and your dog has independently decided to change some of his ways. This canine wake-up call is an example of a dog's innate intelligence; once your pet figures out who's calling the shots (that would be *you*, of course), self-governance kicks in and life gets easier for everyone. Surprise, surprise, you are on your way to owning the perfect dog!

In the Blink of an Eye

I'm used to achieving some pretty fast results with my training system, but occasionally, things happen so fast that even *I* do a double take. A couple asked me to work with their four-year-old Bolognese (yes, it's a dog, not an aged spicy Italian spaghetti sauce). During our initial conversation, the owner described her increasing frustration over the dog's belligerent barking. It seemed like a typical case, but once I came eye-to-eye with the dog, I knew it was much more than that.

This little white powder puff of a pup presented one of the most extreme cases of frenzied, neurotic barking I've ever encountered. The dog was also aggressive in other ways, more than willing to follow through on her threats in the face of a challenge. My scarred boots are a silent souvenir of her initial attack as I stood at the open door, waiting to pass the threshold into her territory.

My wife and kids, who had accompanied me that day, all looked at me with raised eyebrows after witnessing the dog's opening salvo. Even after the woman confined the dog to the farthest room in the house, it was wearisome trying to converse above the noise. Given a brief moment alone, my wife Kaye and I turned to one another, saying in unison, "*This* one could be a bit of a challenge!"

In raised tones, I outlined the problem to the owners and how it could best be overcome. I explained my training philosophy and demonstrated the equipment I would use, and then asked the woman to bring out her dog so we could begin our work. Sometimes I work alone with a problematic dog before bringing in the owners, but in this case, I wanted one of them to take charge straightaway.

My wife and children are often valuable assets when I work with a client, and this day was no exception. They provided ideal subjects for testing the dog because, initially, their mere *presence* on the sofa provoked the dog's rage.

Knowing that my client was prepared to do her part in the process, I asked my eldest son to jump up from where he was seated and walk near the dog. My client knew exactly what she needed to do the moment her dog yapped, and to her credit, the woman executed her pack-leader "nipping" technique very well. To my surprise, the dog became instantly silent, standing still and watching as my son circled the room, giving a halfhearted bark only one more time while we repeatedly tested her with distractions.

I used my younger son as additional bait, but no matter what he did, the dog remained silent. I then brought in our trusty Judah, who had been waiting patiently outside, and asked him to retrieve some toys we tossed only a few feet away from the Bolognese. I knew the dog had already spotted Judah through a window in the room where it had been imprisoned, and my dog's presence had precipitated much of the earlier uproar. But now the former fluffy white terror was indifferent to this strange dog in her castle. Our next step was the big outdoors.

A World of Difference

We took a stroll outside to a neighbor's yard where there were construction workers present, yet instead of barking as she had done earlier that day, the saucy Bolognese ignored them. From the time the training collar was attached around the dog's neck to the time of her last yap, less than a full minute had lapsed, and from then on, she didn't let out a peep. The owners were aghast.

My wife and I were also stunned at this quick conversion. The owners had worked with four other trainers and had tried a multitude of so-called training devices to no avail. And even though I knew in my heart of hearts that the problem was solvable, I certainly expected the dog to put up a lot more resistance than she did.

The Bolognese received much praise following her transformation. Without putting up a fuss, she reassigned herself to the new pack order. No longer was she burdened with the weight of leadership; no longer was it her job to be the brave protector. Her relief was visible. Her eyes softened, and her body relaxed. Finally, she had been released from the strain of all that awesome responsibility. Now, for the first time, the dog was allowed on the back patio, her owners confident that she would no longer harass the neighbors.

From Bondage to Bonding

It saddens me to think about the hounded dog owners who continually tolerate or suffer the misdeeds of their dogs, sometimes to the extreme. I also feel empathy for the dogs that suffer the unintended consequences created by uneducated owners. Granted, most owners love their dogs unconditionally, expecting nothing or very little in return. I encourage my clients to lavish affection on their dogs when it's deserved. Additionally, I urge owners to offer the reward of freedom, but only when the dog respects the owner's authority. It's a case of give and get back.

Owners at first find it ironic that discipline (the setting and enforcing of boundaries) actually enhances the dog-owner bond instead of undercutting it. When the leadership position is in the rightful hands, all parties are then free to enjoy the fruits of a rewarding relationship, and that's what my job is all about.

The Gift of Discipline

Most of us are keenly aware of the fact that children need boundaries. Many parents, while disciplining their kids, will sometimes exclaim in frustration, "This hurts me more than it hurts you!" But they correct and coach, counsel, and sometimes chastise because they care about their children and want the best for them. Perhaps you can relate based on your own childhood, and if you're a parent, you can empathize. I have always felt that the true definition of love is being willing to do what might be emotionally uncomfortable for you, but is ultimately and unquestionably beneficial for the other party. In other words, fairly administered discipline is a clear expression of love.

Let's extend this idea to our beloved pets: once we comprehend how dogs perceive their world, we can exercise the kind of discipline they will easily understand. Just as a pack leader expresses momentary authority, so can we—with the proper training, tools, and application. This is never a cruelty, as the uninformed or ignorant might suggest. In truth, it's a kindness that keeps an eye on the future.

Once again, let us admit that we human beings are emotional creatures, and our feelings can help or hinder us. Responsible dog ownership means relating to our dogs on *their* emotional terms, not ours. We can spend time relaxing or playing with, and praising our dogs, freely expressing our emotions. But when it comes to training, we must balance praise with discipline and keep our feelings out of it.

Just as a parent might do with a child that needs boundaries, we dog owners must do what needs to be done. *We need to apply short-term discipline for long-term results.* That's what the pack leader does, with no feelings of guilt or self-doubt because responsible, consistent discipline is key to keeping the pack safe, healthy, and intact. Here's another way to look at it: when you take the time to properly train your dog, you both have more time for affection, play, and the freedom to explore. Praise and discipline, responsibility, accountability, and *intended* consequence: these elements represent the foundation of my *Perfect Dog*® training method, and they work.

CHAPTER 7

When patterns are broken, new worlds emerge. —Tuli Kupferberg

Making Change

THE RELATIONSHIP BETWEEN a dog and its owner is in many ways like a dance. Watch an owner take a new step that changes the routine, and in return, the dog's behavior will change. Specifically, when an owner suddenly switches from an unintentional follower role to the position of pack leader, there will be a significant shift in the relationship. During this adjustment period, the dog will be discovering its new boundaries, and the owner will be learning to enforce the new rules. People often ask how long it takes for both parties to adapt, and my answer is, "It all depends." The time frame depends on two factors: the owner's consistent and properly executed performance and the dog's personality or strength of will.

Tactic Traps

As you may expect, dogs with subservient personalities will submit more quickly and easily to their owner's new rules, while those with dominant dispositions will more likely resist surrendering their perceived authority. Naturally bold dogs can be quite inventive in their opposition tactics; their cries of objection and attempts at avoidance or even escape can feel overwhelming.

This is the point where owners are tempted to let their emotions run wild and give in to their pet's demands, blinding their vision of what is beneficial in the long term. Strong-willed dogs are like rebellious children who express outrage the first time their parents say an emphatic no and a battle of wills takes place. People need to know that *every* dog has its own resistance threshold and it's a case of waiting it out. Owners must stand firm because there's always a point at which, after some resistance, their dog will cease its challenge and humbly hand over the reins.

Some dogs, as they adjust to their new position in the pack hierarchy, become more subdued, as if they have lost their edge. One might interpret that the dog's spirit has been broken, but this would be a grave mistake. Consider instead that this is yet another deliberate tactic the dog will employ to discourage any further discipline. Who would think a simple canine could be this smart? But dogs can be brilliant when they want to be. Owners need to understand that this self-contained stage is only temporary, and they don't want to reinforce it in any way. If the dog is given too much attention or coddled during this period, all progress will be lost.

Dogs that dig in their heels in quiet defiance are playing an emotional blackmail game similar to pouting children who aren't getting their way. For some owners, this reaction can be more disconcerting than an overt in-your-face defiance, but this form of rebellion must be ignored. Like all dogs, these crafty canines have an end point in their tolerance threshold. When their petulance doesn't yield the results they want, the dogs give in. Every owner needs to understand that while dogs may not be able to think like us, they do know how to devise their own game plan and stick to it. Put simply, many dogs outsmart and outlast their owners in the struggle for who leads the pack, and that's the cold, hard truth.

Even Timid Needs Tender Toughness

Although timidity is not a tactic as such, it's a personality type that can throw owners for a loop. Some excessively passive dogs often find themselves in a predicament where none of their new pack members (their human family) assume the leadership position. In the world of canines, a passive dog would never arise as leader, nor would it ever consider putting up a challenge for leadership. Timid dogs need authority figures in their lives to feel secure. You can probably appreciate how much these dogs struggle when they suddenly find themselves being promoted to an uncomfortably high position in the hierarchy of their new home pack.

Many of these dogs develop a condition called fear aggression, which I discuss in more detail later in this book. As with all forms of aggression, the signs of fear aggression include growling, snarling, and barking—but the set of signals can also include a lowered tail and ears, skulking body position, and measured retreat from the perceived threat. In other words, the dog may sound confident and, at first glance, appear very much in charge. But note the *conflicting* body language; what looks like dominant aggression is actually motivated by fear and insecurity.

Many timid dogs—overwhelmed by their awesome responsibilities— develop neurotic behaviors such as pacing, uncontrolled urination, and incessantly chewing their own body parts. While the symptoms of overwhelm may vary widely, there's one thing these timid dogs in big boots have in common: they would welcome someone, anyone, to fill their shoes and rescue them from the emotional burden of unwanted leadership.

Given this counterintuitive insight, you can imagine how destructive it is when owners react to fear aggression or neurotic behaviors by coddling and being overprotective of their poor pooch. Of course, this only exacerbates the timidity problem. Owners fear that any kind of discipline will send their dog "off the rails," so they back off instead of enforcing boundaries. Yet caring firmness is the answer to the problem, not leniency.

Supersensitive dogs want and need a leader who will confidently take the reins no matter how their pet may initially react. The timid dog needs straightforward instruction, coherent correction, and a clear sense of its position in the pack, and well-defined praise and play. In time, shy dogs are able to shelve their cautions and concerns as they look to their leader as a source of confidence and stability.

King of the Hill

If you have any doubts about how establishing clear authority over your dog will greatly enhance your relationship, here's a superb demonstration of how a dog will actively seek favor from even the most hard-nosed leader. One afternoon I took Judah for an outing at a local dog park where I planned to shoot some filler footage for my TV show. I was looking for examples of doggie disobedience and mischief that typically happen in such places. Judah, the irrepressible Mr. Social Guy, darted here and there, befriending as many dogs as he could the minute we entered the park.

As Judah bounded and played with various dogs, a large, "studly" boxer and his owner sauntered into the park, slowly heading toward a small pavilion near where I was standing. Absorbed with capturing video footage for my show, I was only slightly aware that Judah had stopped by to check in with me. Then Judah noticed the boxer, and he immediately approached the bigger dog, hoping to find someone new to play with.

With a fierce display of aggression, the boxer slammed Judah to the ground and held him there by his neck. Judah lay there in complete submission, offering no resistance whatsoever, just as I had trained him to do for his own safety. You are probably aware that responding in kind to an aggressor only causes an attack to escalate, placing the defending dog at potential risk. I yelled, hoping to startle the boxer, while the owner pulled his dog away. The young man apologized to me as Judah, shaken but resilient, rose to his feet and returned to playing with the other dogs.

But a few seconds later, Judah returned to the scene of his previous humbling. He again approached the boxer in the same friendly, nonthreatening manner, and was once again immediately pounced upon. The boxer's owner retrieved his beast once more and, like watching an instant replay, Judah ran off to play with the dogs that were waiting for him to return.

You might find this surprising, but Judah returned for a *third* round, this time displaying an almost comical but very telling display of the nature and workings of canine society. This time, Judah approached the boxer very slowly, in an exaggerated cowering stance, with his hind end almost dragging on the ground. With his ears back and head down, cocked at an angle, Judah crept up from the side, slightly behind the boxer, while licking gingerly toward the dog's face. Judah was clearly communicating to the boxer that he was in no way a threat to the dog's dominance.

With this new approach, the boxer accepted Judah's presence and began to march slowly around with Judah close to his side. My dog continued holding his submissive stature, but with each step that both dogs took, he gradually returned to his normal upright profile. Within thirty seconds, Judah had relaxed. He began initiating small signals of playfulness toward his former antagonist. The two dogs were now behaving as if there had never been an issue between them.

The Calm after the Storm

There is much to be learned from this interaction. Judah had all the opportunity in the world to keep his distance from the boxer after that first overpowering introduction. There were a dozen dogs in the park that were willing to romp with him. Yet Judah chose to return to the boxer a second time, and even a third. Anyone watching this scene might have surmised that Judah had forgotten what happened the first time, but that's not what was going on. Judah's third approach demonstrated a dog's thought processes, shedding light on how the social environment within which dogs operate is so very different from that of human beings.

Judah recognized the power and authority this boxer presented, and given the choice, he chose to bond. Judah sacrificed his playmates and willingly submitted himself to a potential third chastening so he might establish a strong and respectful connection with the clear leader of the park. Judah wanted and needed the boxer's acceptance, despite the alpha dog's initial aggressiveness. Perhaps you find this story surprising or insightful; a lot of people do. It offers a profound example of how dogs view the world.

I'm sure you took note of Judah's submissive posture during his third approach. This left no doubt in the boxer's mind what Judah's intentions were. Judah's body language was an obvious expression of subservience that left no doubt as to which dog held the dominant position. I like to tell my clients this story because dogs often use similar body language when they are presented with an authoritative training method for the first time.

If you have a similar experience with your dog, it's absolutely critical for you to understand that it isn't a "bad thing" when your trainee dog cowers or offers pathetic-looking signs of submission in response to commands and corrections. You're not a monster and you're not being mean—you're simply being clear on who the leader is. Don't let guilt or self-doubt cause you to back away from your position of authority; remind yourself that these behaviors are an excellent sign that the training is working.

Rest assured, as your dog learns to confidently self-govern within its new boundaries, your pet will become more relaxed, just as my dog did. Judah returned to his normal playful self once the pack dynamics with the boxer got sorted out. Judah's submissive posture was short lived, and once the two dogs had established their positions in the hierarchy, Judah was no longer subjected to the boxer's enforcement of dominion. The two dogs could interact without threat, and Judah was free to come and go as he pleased.

Work Like a Dog

When I describe Judah's second round of harsh treatment, I love to ask people if they think my dog would approach the boxer a third time, and the answer is always no. They expect that Judah would choose to be safe and simply play with his "buddies." Let's face it; this is how most human beings (emotional creatures that we are) would react if another person treated us so harshly. But as you know, we can't assess the interaction between Judah and the boxer on human terms.

No matter how well behaved, darling, or intelligent they are, dogs are not human beings. Dogs have an innate, wired-in need to operate within an orderly hierarchical environment. They must either lead or be led; they don't function well in an inconsistent or ambiguous environment. The dominance and discipline established by a pack leader provides the much-needed emotional stability pack members seek. In turn, the leader earns the respect, affection, and appreciation of its members.

Too many dog owners perceive that firm, clear, consistent discipline (unkindly called compulsion training by those who disapprove) will break a dog's spirit. Many owners like to believe that dogs should be allowed to freely express their instinctive desires (whatever they are), and to do otherwise constitutes an oppressed creature. By now, you know what I say to this absurd way of thinking!

Shifting Gears

Regardless of its personality type, when the parameters of a dog's life are changed, it needs time to make the mental shift, to reprogram itself according to which behaviors are allowed and which are not. Whether the dog initially reacts with raucous rebellion, silent stubbornness, or tries to retreat into its world of imaginary fears, the end result is always the same as long as the owner stays the course. It's inevitable that the dog will make mistakes (or more appropriately, unwise choices) during this period of adjustment. He will be a little uncertain, and perhaps a little bewildered, until all of the new rules are established in his mind. The owner can help the dog avoid confusion by communicating in a consistent, clear, and confident manner. This means using the appropriate words and body language with each separate command so the dog can sort it all out.

Once the dog understands and accepts the revised "law of the land," it will adapt; obedience will become the default mode, and the dog will be on its way to self-governance. Here's the payoff for everyone: once the dog fully accepts its owner as the pack leader and the ultimate source of authority, the relationship will strengthen and deepen. As trust and confidence increase, the long-term bond takes root and grows.

An Exercise in Leadership

Here's a subject few people think about when introducing new rules and enhanced discipline, so let's get it out there for you loud and clear—*make sure you provide adequate physical exercise for your dog.* You can seriously undermine your training success if you fail to give your dog the exercise it needs. Regular vigorous play sessions are a critical part of bonding with your dog and working through your mutual issues so your pet isn't tempted to expend its pent-up energy in troublesome ways.

Although "regular" will vary according to the breed, age, and condition of your dog, I generally recommend at least two twenty-minute sessions of hard running per day—one in the morning and another in the evening. For my dogs, this typically involves chasing and retrieving a ball. By the way, a walk around the block or even a two-hour-long walk every day doesn't equate to *quality* exercise. If you like to walk with your dog, that's fine, but don't think you're fulfilling your dog's exercise needs with a mere walk unless he's very old or legitimately incapacitated.

Your attempts to train or retrain your dog and correct undesirable behaviors will be unsuccessful if your dog simply redirects its energy into mischief making. If your dog lacks sufficient exercise, you'll simply be trading one problem for another because he'll resort to annoying or destructive behaviors out of sheer frustration. If you do supply your dog a suitable energy outlet, you won't have to suffer any pangs of guilt by having to admit you're part of the problem and not part of the solution.

Proper exercise is an integral ingredient in achieving your end goal of a well-trained dog. As a responsible owner, it's your job to provide your pet not only with food, shelter, and safety, but the freedom to run, explore, fetch, and play without the need for physical restraint. Your willingness to lead the way is the key to the long-term companionship you both will enjoy: this is the ultimate reward of effective training.

Lessons from a Pack Leader

I counsel my clients *never* to believe that they must endure the dire consequences of bad dog behavior—lifelong disobedience and rebellion are not part of a dog pack's natural order. And responsible, consistent discipline will not quell a dog's spirit. In the social structure of a dog pack, the kinds of bad behaviors owners too often tolerate are *not* a daily occurrence between the leader and his subordinates.

Misbehavior and acts of disobedience are simply not permitted in a pack because they disrupt order and harmony. Unlike many human owners, the alpha dog is quick to subdue any behavior that pushes his buttons. Nor does the pack leader put up with acts of aggression from any subordinate. Peace and cooperation are maintained through the ongoing application of discipline—the essential ingredient that allows the pack to not just survive, but thrive.

When we, as responsible owners, step up to the plate and operate as dependable pack leaders, we make it crystal clear that certain behaviors will not be tolerated. When we employ appropriate, steadfast discipline, our dog's bad behaviors will cease, paving the way for fewer moments of frustration or displeasure, and more time for love, companionship, and playfulness. After all, isn't that the reason why we have our pets in the first place?

CHAPTER 8

*A great deal of intelligence can be invested in ignorance
when the need for illusion is deep.* —Saul Bellow

Fortune and Fame

THE MEDIA PLAYS a major role in how we perceive the role of dogs in our lives. Disney and others have produced countless movies featuring sappy, sentimental portrayals of dogs as heroes, victims, or outlaws. Whether the on-screen dog is pure and obedient, downtrodden and neglected, or mischievous and roguish, each possesses endearing qualities. There is never any backstory about how the good dog became good, and nothing is ever done to correct the naughty dog. It all just "is." Whether watching an animation or a movie depiction, we predictably see the full cast of characters living in blissful acceptance of whatever happens all the way to the sweet or bittersweet end.

So what does it take to create the perfect movie dog? It takes a *lot* of them! For example, the magnificent Lassie of the TV series was portrayed by not one, but five dogs. The engaging Eddie from the popular show *Frazier* involved three dogs performing their individual tricks, lending the impression that Jack Russell terriers are spunky little love bundles of endless energy and entertainment.

When children grow up watching romanticized portrayals of dogs, they can't help but be influenced by what they see (this includes you and me). From *Old Yeller, Lassie, Rin Tin Tin, 101 Dalmatians,* and *Beethoven* to *My Dog Skip* and the all-time star of doggie mischief, *Marley*—this is a small sampling of the mind-altering subject matter that has indoctrinated generations of would-be dog owners. These idealized depictions of dog ownership prompt many to impulsively exclaim those life-changing words: "Let's get a dog!"

Lest you think I'm overstating my case, every time *101 Dalmatians* hits the screen, sales of that breed skyrocket. But sadly, as the puppies mature, high numbers of Dalmatians are dumped off at the dog pound as disheartened owners learn the hard way that this breed doesn't automatically make an ideal family pet. It might be insightful for you to take a moment and consider the childhood impressions you formed about dogs by recalling your favorite canine "stars" and how you were influenced by their characterizations.

Buy the Way

Pick up any doggie magazine or go to a pet store and you will be inundated with options and accessories promulgating the fine art of pooch pampering. Corporations and businesses catering to the dog industry know they can count on indulgent owners to project human need onto their pets. In other words, dogs are depicted as having the same materialistic wants and needs as their human counterparts.

From the local mom-and-pop shop to mega corporations, the pet industry generates about forty billion dollars a year in sales. If this were simply an example of an active market strengthening a national economy, there would be no need for concern. But a rational person has to wonder if dogs really need to be dressed up for Halloween or other holidays, if they need birthday parties, beauty contests, bling, and piles of toys so towering they outweigh the dog.

Perhaps we should err on the side of caution and consider that there may be unexamined consequences connected to this dollar-driven frenzy, and if we step back, we can investigate what exactly is going on. We need to ask ourselves what kind of effect such extreme owner self-indulgence has on pets. What if we spent less time spoiling our dogs and more time training them? What if we were less quick to condemn training methods we don't understand and more inclined to educate ourselves about what it truly means to be an effective pet owner in the long term?

If you were to have any difficulty answering these kinds of questions, then you might want to investigate the history of your conditioning. Often the culprit isn't just the information we readily see and hear, but also what is deliberately and conveniently withheld from us, the public.

Doggin' It

For the first season of my national Canadian TV show *Doggin' It*, we filmed the standard thirteen episodes. As soon as the first episode was aired, I started gaining a strong fan base and receiving e-mails from viewers all across the country stating that my show was the best dog-related program they had seen. People were amazed at how I could work with a problem dog in just seven minutes and dramatically change its behavior. Some had quit their dog obedience classes because they were getting better results from the techniques they saw on my show than through their weeks of formal lessons. We continued being flooded with positive e-mails and letters following each episode, but after the last segment aired, the enthusiasm took an unexpected turn.

Silence Is Golden

This episode's training segment involved a cute ten-week-old golden retriever puppy that was keeping its owners up all night with screams of protest against being placed in a training kennel, or cage. These were no small whimpers or whines, but nonstop bellows and bawls, and everyone in the family was losing precious sleep. They had tried all kinds of suggestions from friends and family, but to no avail. As a desperate measure, the frustrated wife resorted to sleeping on the floor in front of the dog's cage every night because this was the only way their little terror would shut up! This is yet another pathetic example of how people let their dogs train them instead of the other way around.

As was the case with most of my show guests, I had not met the woman or her pup before our segment—allowing me to achieve unrehearsed, real-time results. I wanted viewers to see how easily and quickly this type of problem could be resolved. With the cameras rolling, I placed the pup in its training kennel and then moved behind a wall near the cage's corner so the golden couldn't see me (the camera was positioned to capture both of us). As soon as I closed the cage door, the feisty little pup let loose with its deafening demands to be let out.

Still in my hiding place, I explained above the din that from the time her puppies are born, a mother dog introduces them to the concept of consequences. If she's pleased with her offspring's behavior, all is well and the babies can relish in her affection and the freedom she allows. If the mother is displeased with any one of her pups, she applies appropriate physical discipline, depending on its age and the nature of its misbehavior.

Her correction is a nudge or a nip, an instinctive response aimed at maintaining the pack order, which is critical to survival. The mother dog will be just forceful enough to let her baby know a behavior change is required, but gentle enough to do no harm. One pup might be more stubborn than another and, thus, will require firmer handling, yet each has its own learning threshold where it submits to the mother's authority. My point is that even a *tiny* puppy soon figures out that continued disobedience is simply not worth the corrective consequences.

In Your Face

As the retriever pup's tantrum continued, I simulated a mother dog's disciplinary maneuver, reaching around and squirting him with water from a spray bottle. I said "Quiet!" in a firm tone before disappearing behind the wall again. I explained to my viewers that this might have to be done several times, consistently and persistently, before the pup decides it would rather quiet down than continue being sprayed. Just as I expected, this strong-willed youngster continued his demanding cries. Once again, I moved out of my hiding spot and squirted a few good shots of water through a gap in the cage wire while repeating my "quiet" command.

I then explained to my audience that it helps to use a systematic escalation of disciplinary tactics if a defiant doggie doesn't respond to a simple method such as water correction. This means you slowly increase the level of discipline if at first you don't get your desired results. For example, if the spraying strategy doesn't work, a frustrated owner could try a muzzle or corrective training collar. For every dog's safety, I always caution that a pet should *never* be left unattended when any kind of physical device is being used.

As my seven-minute segment rolled to an end, the camera zoomed in on the puppy, now curled up into a bundle of cuteness, sleeping peacefully in its cage. This was the only time the pup had ever fallen asleep in the training kennel since the day the owners had brought him home.

This welcome result had been quickly accomplished with a few squirts of water and a series of vocal commands. The amazed and relieved owners confided that none of the training advice they'd been given had been so simple—or successful. I had clearly shown the pup that he would not win this battle of wills; that there was no way he'd be let out of the cage. Once the pup realized who was in charge, it accepted the situation and fell asleep in minutes. The owner was overjoyed that she and her family could now regain some semblance of order and peace in their lives.

Uncaged Outrage

After this episode aired, I came head to head with the dark side of the activist mind-set. We received some e-mails from viewers who were self-described animal lovers, but they certainly weren't in love with me—or my methods! The radical tirades, threats, and outright hatred they expressed threw me for a loop. In their eyes I was mean, cruel, twisted, abusive, and loathsome. It was hard to believe the level of hostility these people hurled at me.

Reading these angry, fuming diatribes, I realized what I had done. I had demonized the sacred. I had ventured where no dog trainer had gone before. I had disciplined an angelic, innocent little puppy! I had taken the representation of all that is good in our world and dared insist that a defenseless puppy be held accountable for its actions. I had taken the "essence of innocence" and ravaged it in the name of discipline. You would have thought I had committed a crime worthy of death.

There were fewer than two dozen e-mails, but some of them were so filled with violent tones, I began wondering if I should be concerned for my personal safety and that of my family. One message was so disturbing, I called the police and read it over the phone, concerned that the writer might act on his threats. It blew my mind to consider how someone can profess to love an animal, yet display such hatred and disregard for a human life in the same breath. Go figure!

The show's sponsors received a few complaint calls too—not just in Canada where the show was aired, but also in the U.S. where the parent company is located. Some of the protests were from people who had *never even seen* the episode, nor were they familiar with the series. These protesters had been simply swept away by inflammatory chatter and felt they had to vent their second-hand indignation. You could have predicted what happened next. Despite the hundreds of letters and e-mails we had received from all of the previous episodes, the smattering of missives and phone calls complaining about the puppy segment carried the most weight for the sponsor.

Backing Off, Backing Down

At first, the producers of the show told me not to worry about the negative comments. They were used to people griping about certain programs now and then. But when the backlash made it all the way to the parent company in the U.S., our Canadian sponsor scheduled a conference call. So here I was, sitting in the TV station boardroom with the show's producer and executive producer, discussing the issue with the two sponsor representatives. They were dog owners themselves. They had watched the training segment in question and had seen nothing objectionable from a personal point of view.

However, the man in charge of risk assessment felt that the company's brand name could be damaged if they didn't do something to appease the offended viewers. It was decided that we needed to reshoot the segment to remove any potential offensive imagery or information. Apparently, any kind of discipline imposed on a cute, cuddly puppy was considered too controversial; and the last thing the sponsor wanted was a public relations incident.

The sponsor wasn't concerned about the validity of the message I was presenting. After all, the people who saw the episode without pushing the panic button appreciated the astounding fact that a ten-week-old puppy can be disciplined quickly and effectively.

But the sponsor fixated on public perception of the company's brand and the need to preserve its *image*. They wanted to be perceived across the board as a "feel-good" company that cares for animals so consumers would continue buying their products.

As we all know, the real job of a corporation is to make as much money for the shareholders as possible. What *really* works for dogs and their owners plays a distant second to the corporation's first concern: the bottom line. In short, programming drives profits. Although the show producers reassured the sponsor that the complaints would die down, our having to reshoot the piece was, to me, a blatant form of commercial censorship. To the sponsor, it was merely PR.

The PR Pretext

I tell this story because it's one small example of the behind-the-scenes machinations that can alter the content of a media product and influence consumers. Though I was treated like a criminal by the perpetrators of the hate mail I received, to me the real crime was that an important and practical message was censored from the viewing public because of the emotional, irrational rants of a vocal, largely uninformed minority.

By all means, this wasn't the first time I witnessed a PR whitewash, and it won't be the last. Perhaps you recall the media's alarmingly casual coverage of an orca trainer's near drowning at Sea World, San Diego, in 2006. Just as my TV show sponsors censored information that could help owners establish safer dog-owner relationships, Sea World deliberately concealed information that could have potentially saved lives. The tragedy is that in both cases, facts were suppressed for the sake of corporate revenue.

Some people might say it's a stretch comparing a belligerent puppy being squirted with water to a giant orca nearly drowning a trainer, but here's the parallel: when vital information is covered up, there can be huge consequences. You see, properly taming a dominant dog when it's young will virtually eliminate any potential for the dog to attack once it's grown. Every interaction you and your pack members have with your dog is part of the complete package of respect you must seek to gain and maintain. So when information that could prevent your dog from gaining the upper hand is deliberately kept from you, the potential for harm significantly increases.

In the world of PR, illusion always overshadows information or evidence. And while we're on the subject, let's take on the granddaddy of them all: the Westminster Kennel Club Dog Show. We're talking big-time media, enormous influence, the emphasis on appearances, and mega money. If you want to lay your eyes on the capstone of the canine illusion contrivance and all its trappings, look no further.

All That Glitters Is Not Gold

Established in 1877, the annual Westminster Dog Show is a two-day benched conformation show held in New York City's Madison Square Garden. Dog owners from around the world come to show their ultra-bred, ultra-groomed, pick-of-the-litter pooches, judged closely by eminent AKC (American Kennel Club) judges.

It sounds top drawer, prestigious, and powerful—and it is. But there's an underbelly that goes far beyond picture-perfect dogs with gleaming coats, flawless conformation, and poise. That these show dogs have impeccable pedigrees is indisputable, but there's an underlying and grossly incorrect assumption that exceptional bloodlines equate to excellent behavior. In other words, it's all about appearance. What I perceive as a glaring omission is never questioned by the audience, the media, or those involved in the show; all parties seem content to share the delusion that these dazzling doggies are perfect in every way. Nothing could be farther from the truth.

If you could sneak a peek behind the curtains of this notorious event and into the homes of some contestants, you'd see the awful truth. A high percentage of those primped, pampered canines are not the well-mannered, self-possessed pups they appear to be, and no one seems to care. To put it bluntly, many of the show dogs get away with murder because their primary function is to look good, not be good. The Little Shop of Show Horrors includes runaway rogues, boisterous barkers, jittery jumpers, demolition divas, and more—just like everywhere else.

"But how could this be?" some may ask in bewilderment. "They seem so wonderfully well behaved out there in the ring!" Yes, they do, but only because they have been bribed and bedazzled with treats to follow a precise routine for a scant few minutes, all the while restrained by a tightly held leash. This is not obedience; it's performance. It's about putting on a show.

There are pound dogs and purebreds that can perform extraordinary tricks. They can complete an obstacle course in record time, play flawless Fly Ball, catch all kinds of objects in midair, and conquer other agility-type events. But as soon as their event is over, they run amok, and it's the same story at home.

I don't know about you, but I'd rather have an ordinary, untalented dog that just happens to be the most well-behaved mutt in the neighborhood. To me, there should be ribbons for that kind of performance. It's not that I have anything against tricks or fine features. I've taught all of my dogs many fun games as a means of keeping them stimulated and for strengthening my bond with them, but these activities have never taken preeminence over day-to-day obedience.

Best in Show

Some new clients feel compelled to rattle off their dog's show history, as if an impressive pedigree or collection of trophies guarantees good behavior or trainability. From the most basic local conformation contests to the bigger regional shows, certain people just can't help themselves, hinting or overtly mentioning all the money they spend to show off their special pooch. But I know where their drive comes from. The Westminster Dog Show and others like it always attract a good deal of media attention, inspiring many a purebred dog owner to harbor dreams of such lofty heights.

The highlight of the Westminster competition, of course, is the *Best in Show* title—a term you're most likely familiar with. Attaining such a prize earns the dog and its owner instant fame as they are paraded through the media circuit. Sponsors swing into action, offering the perfect pair lucrative advertising contracts. Sales of the winning breed swell, and the individual canine winner turns into a breeding goldmine.

While the Westminster spectacle is a bit "highbrow" for the owner of an average family pet, many people enjoy reading and hearing about this mysterious world of canine celebrity. Think again of the child we once were, poised in our theater seat watching Lassie and the other heroic dogs, wishing we could have a piece of the action. Well, Westminster is the adult equivalent.

How Unfortunate

One of the most misleading and destructive parts of Westminster Fever is the attention paid to self-proclaimed canine mystics. Throughout the event,

71

media headlines are abuzz about contestants clamoring for advice from prominent dog psychics. Yes, dog psychics! These presumptuous people fancy that they are gifted with the ability to read a dog's mind so they can provide the owners with intriguing insights and inside secrets about their pet.

In addition to discussing a dog's potential for a ribbon, the dog psychic supposedly identifies a dog's likes and dislikes, so owners can better know their pet. Brace yourself, there's more: owners are encouraged to believe that their dog's less-than-desirable behaviors are a need for self-expression. An unruly dog might be labeled "spunky" or "spirited," but the concepts of boundaries or accountability are never mentioned.

If you're finding this hard to swallow, join the club. Yet there are more owners than you could imagine who wait in line for consultations and pay a hefty fee for such "services." And then there are the fans that want to read about it. Ah, human nature!

Sometimes the reports are amusing. One article noted a show dog's embarrassing declaration that he couldn't stand the way his owner smelled when the man returned home from work, requesting that the owner please take a shower straightaway. Yes, this is a true story, but I propose that perhaps the *mystic* found the owner's odor offensive and decided there was a way to address this sensitive issue by way of a public service.

Smelly armpits aside, when serious acts of doggie defiance are defended or dismissed by people in positions of perceived authority, I get agitated. Once again, an unsuspecting dog owner is swayed toward permissiveness and indulgence, thanks to a psychic's persuasive accounts of why the dog is moved to behave this way or that.

The underlying message of all these articles is that *true* dog lovers accept bad behaviors from their dogs with a shake of the head and a dismissing chuckle. After all, who would dare question the impeccable image of Westminster and all of those well-dressed, impressionable owners so deeply immersed in the world of dog shows?

And there again is the operative word: image. From illusionary PR campaigns that distort the facts to costly competitive events that measure the wrong qualities, it's easy to get sucked into a parallel universe that promotes superficial standards because it's founded on fortune, fame, or both. Let's be real. Effective dog training is not about appearances; it's about *actions*.

CHAPTER 9

The belly can rule the mind. ~ *Latin Proverb*

"What it really comes down to is a question of values... Is a delicious, succulent turkey, baked to perfection, worth a few whacks on the nose with a newspaper?"

Not-So-Sweet Solutions

THERE IS BIG money to be made in the doggie-biscuit business. The manufacturers of dog treats will apply the best of their marketing magic to lure you into indulging your dog with their delicious delicacies. The sponsor of my Canadian television show was a manufacturer of dog food and treats, and their marketing practices proved in no uncertain terms where their loyalties lay.

Consider the weight of social pressures that exist in ads, images, and articles suggesting that dog lovers are obligated to liberally dish out the treats. After all, aren't tempting tidbits a perfect way for owners to express love and devotion to their dogs? Consequently, when I criticize the practice of tasty tidbits as rewards, people tend to look at me as if my hair is on fire. I know they're wondering what could possibly be wrong with a little bit of pooch pampering.

I strongly object to spoiling or bribing dogs with food because it automatically places the giver in a subordinate position. Consider that if you drop a piece of meat in the middle of three untrained dogs, you will immediately see a display of dominance or overt aggression to win that food. Dogs are willing to *fight* for food, and any dog that backs off and surrenders food to another is considered a follower. So every time you hand your dog a morsel from your plate, guess what message you're reinforcing in his mind? Yes, you are telling your dog, "Here is my gift for you, oh mighty pack leader. I respect you. Take my food. I am your follower."

Not only are you giving away your power, you're also setting an inconvenient and potentially dangerous precedent for any person who should ever interact with your pet. Your dog will quickly learn to assume that human beings are by nature passive, submissive, and willing to readily relinquish one of the staples of life that canines are prepared to vie for. So it should come as no surprise if one day your dog slams a neighbor's child to the ground in pursuit of her ice cream cone. Maybe the damage will be confined to a bruised knee and a few tears, but what if the child puts up a struggle? In this situation, the dog is merely attempting to procure what it feels entitled to based on its experience of being hand-fed. But with the wrong person at the wrong time, the results could be disastrous.

Good Intentions, Bad Results

If it's been your tendency to bestow bellyfuls of bounty upon your four-legged buddy, my intention is not to insult you but to offer insight as to why it's not a productive practice. Most people have no clue as to how treat giving is viewed by the canine brain. Because owners offer treats as an act of affection, they assume that food is *received* in the same vein. This is another example of human beings projecting their feelings, instincts, and motivations on their pet instead of trying to comprehend the canine perspective. The rationale is simple and oh so well-intended: receiving edibles and other gifts from someone is an endearing act; the giver earns our favor. Therefore, if we freely give tasty tidbits to our dogs then they will love us more.

But let me state again: love is not respect, and respect is what we need to first establish. Love automatically follows respect, and it grows exponentially. As your dog's respect for you deepens, so too does his love; this is an unconditional, enduring love that is far superior to the superficial affection that a treat-obsessed dog develops for its follower.

The subject of dog treats and food as love is a personal and complex one, but my point is that neither dogs nor their owners are benefiting from the practice. The only party that really benefits is the manufacturer.

A Typical Tale About Treats

Sad to say, treats have become an almost automatic part of puppy procurement. Perhaps you can relate to the following scenario that I've deliberately embellished, but only a bit.

A couple decides to get a new pup. They spend endless hours researching breeds to find one that fits their likes and lifestyle, but they can't find one that exactly meets their criteria. They throw all their research out the door and bring home the cutest puppy they see, falling head over heels with the little snuggle muffin once they look into those big brown eyes and hold it in their arms.

Determined to be responsible owners, the couple makes an appointment with the veterinarian to check the pup over and give its first set of shots. Upon arrival at the clinic, the couple and their new addition are greeted by a gaggle of swooning receptionists and veterinary assistants, all of whom go gaga over the gorgeous little munchkin. The unsuspecting owners are about to be formally initiated into the Cookie Club. The password by established members is "May I give your dog a treat?" To which the answer must be a resounding "Certainly!" Saying no is an insult that will forever bar you from being an official member of this prestigious group.

Before leaving the vet's office, the couple is invited to join a puppy kindergarten class where they will learn how to be good "parents" and make lasting friendships with other new mommies and daddies. They will organize birthday parties, doggie playdates, and reunions for their furry offspring while sipping their Starbucks and sharing favorite photos.

On the first day of kindergarten, all the owners dutifully bring a bag of recommended treats to stimulate their puppy's readiness to learn (they may even have been cautioned to not feed their pups before class). The first lesson might involve teaching puppies how to socialize with strangers: the owners all stand in a circle, passing their puppy off to the person on their right. As the pups work their way around the circle, they are given a treat from each new person they meet, with the intent of demonstrating that human beings are friendly creatures and nice to be around. The pups are generally more than happy to oblige as they receive munchies from each human hand.

At home, the owners continue luring their pups into obedience by offering a treat for every good deed performed just as they were instructed to do by the puppy kindergarten guru. Despite the struggles they may experience in sometimes holding their pup's attention or running up against a show of stubbornness, the new owners dare not question the wisdom of their teacher. The pup quickly clues into the "treat game," masterfully manipulating the hearts of its new pack members with token performances of "sit," "stay," and "come," eagerly expecting that yet another reward will be forthcoming.

At first, the pup is content to placate his two-legged playmates and gobble his gourmet gifts, but boredom soon ensues, and he finds more interesting things to explore. Out come the slippers. The couch leg becomes a chew toy. The open door beckons, and the garbage smells irresistible. The owners, once so delighted with their pup, are now desperate because food morsels no longer motivate their pampered pooch. They escalate from the once-revered dry dog biscuits to tasty table food, but that too is eventually rejected for something more satisfying like chasing the cat or tampering with the roll of toilet paper. Thus, the pathway to chaos has been paved.

Love Is only as Deep as the Cookie Jar Is Full

Here's a perfect example of how shallow the river of love runs in a treat-filled world. A woman asked me to train her two dogs, a six-year-old Bouvier and a five-year-old Jack Russell terrier. Both dogs had aggression issues, and living with them had become a nightmare. Even a short drive in the car left the owner utterly exhausted as her dogs leaped about the vehicle, barking incessantly at whatever came their way.

On the first day of training, I counseled the woman that absolutely no treats would be given to her dogs. This woman was wealthy. She lived in a beautiful home with a good deal of land; there was even a caretaker's cottage on her property, inhabited by a dog-loving couple. The daily routine consisted of feeding the dogs their dinner at the main home, after which the dogs would go visit the caretakers for dessert and a "love fest."

The dogs would be greeted with abundant enthusiasm and an equal amount of treats. Thanks to this long-held tradition, the caretakers felt loved and appreciated, and so did their two furry friends (or so the caretakers thought). All appeared well and wonderful in the land of Doggiedom.

The owner promised that everyone would abide by the new "no-treat" rule without exception, but later in the week, she reported that the caretakers were sad and confused because "The dogs aren't coming to visit us anymore!" It only took two days for the dogs to realize there were no more handouts at the home of the caretakers. Once the palatable pattern had been broken, the dogs dropped their benefactors like hot potatoes because the core of the dogs' affection had been based on full bellies. This is an excellent example of how we human beings so easily misinterpret appetite for allegiance and how superficial a dog's so-called love can be when it's based on food.

A Bone to Pick

Perhaps you may be thinking, "But I don't train my dog with treats. I might offer a few scraps now and then, but certainly there's no harm in that!" Let's begin this discussion by agreeing that using food as reward for your dog's obedience or good behavior is out-and-out bribery. Well, successful training involves changing the core of your dog's being so he heeds the boundaries you set—not because he's being paid off but because he unquestionably respects you. And there's more.

Training a dog is far more than showing up for scheduled sessions in a specific location. Dog training is a 24/7 process. It begins the moment your new dog steps foot inside your car for that first trip home, and it ends with your dog's last breath. My point is that even though you may not use treats as a reward when teaching, for example, the "down" command, the minute you hand him a scrap from the cutting board as he parks near your feet in the kitchen, you have taught your dog a lesson. Your pet has learned he can use his presence to subtly coerce you into feeding him.

Even though your puppy may know all the commands and obey all the house rules by the time he's six months old, his continued obedience for the rest of his lifetime reflects the foundation of training you have established. Should you at any point lapse into exception mode (such as feeding him scraps from the table), the training will take a different course. Your dog will quickly transform into a manipulative beggar who uses a forlorn face, pleading eyes, or a pitiful whine as weapons to melt your heart.

Owners that say they don't use treats to train their dogs need to know that every piece of food that leaves their hand and makes its way into their dog's mouth represents an opportunity for the dog to disrespect the owner's position of leadership. Does this mean that you can *never* feed your dog anything other than regular dog food? Does it mean that you can never toss your dog a bone or offer a treat? The answer is essentially no, but you need to be very cautious about how you dish out the extras.

Your dog's food bowl must become the dispenser for *all* edibles, at times of the day that only you determine. This creates a separation between you and the food. Even bones can be presented this way, whether inside or outside the house. You also set a good training precedent by approaching your dog and being nearby while he's eating. You can even remove his dinner or bone halfway through the meal, provided you practice the safety techniques detailed in my system. When your dog readily surrenders the food he so savors with no signs of aggression, you're well on the way to establishing leadership.

In the Name of Love

There are some dog owners who are so deprived of fulfillment in their own lives, they turn to their dogs to meet their emotional void. Every treat they bestow upon their beloved pet puts purpose and meaning into their lives. These owners might know at an intellectual level that their devotion is unhealthy, but that doesn't mean they will stop. The overfed, unexercised, overweight dog might waddle around the house like a bloated walrus, but the owner continues to regard food as a sign of unparalleled adoration.

Then there are owners who regularly use dog food and treats in an attempt to appease their own guilty consciences, similar to overbusy parents who lavish gifts on their neglected kids to compensate for the parents' lack of presence. Like human beings, a dog will often eat out of boredom, and it's a known fact that the majority of urban dogs suffer from a lack of exercise.

As I state earlier in this book, one or two walks a day isn't enough, even if they're long ones. Dogs need to run and play vigorously so they can feel physically satisfied and mentally stimulated. Too many people fail to take this into consideration when they choose to become dog owners, and down the road, they end up enduring the frustrating consequences. Digging, chewing, barking, jumping, and begging are just some of the many symptoms of a dog suffering from too little exercise. Suffice to say that food rewards are never an acceptable substitute for lack of attention, and they exacerbate the problem of not getting enough exercise.

Finally, there are the owners who perceive they're giving their dogs the highest of honors by sharing human food with their pet. Please don't get me wrong. I commend all owners who do their best to provide their dogs nourishing meals, but I'm impatient with owners who feel pangs of regret or guilt if they don't share their delicious dinner with their pet. Here's the bottom line: human beings don't need dog food, and dogs don't need human food. It's that simple. The owners I describe here need to know that by feeding their pet human food, they are teaching their dogs to be manipulative. How many times have you witnessed or heard about a dog stealthily stealing his owner's sandwich from the table or boosting a piece of roast beef from the cutting board?

The quickest way to turn a dog into a garbage hound or a dumpster diver is to saturate its senses with human food. Yet many owners merely shake their head at their dog's tendency to root in the wastebasket. I say wake up and smell the garbage! If the average dog could open a refrigerator, I would be inundated with calls about how to keep them out, but few people make the connection about why their dog is attracted to the trash.

Go for the Gold

After counseling my clients about treats and the practice of not using food as an expression of love, I'm often asked what an informed owner should do, and here's my answer. When it comes to food, you want to be capable of putting full trust in your dog. This means that even in your absence, your dog will resist the temptation to touch any edibles outside of his doggie dish. When you can rely on your dog to self-govern in this mature and responsible way, you know you have his deepest respect. It is indeed a proud moment when you witness your canine buddy ignoring some savory, scintillating smell hovering right in front of his nose because you've established that it's absolutely and totally off limits.

If you question that this is even possible, here's an example. I had taken Judah to a client's house to help me with distraction lessons while I worked with the owner's three problem dogs. Toward the evening, we decided to test the three dogs on a walk, and I left Judah at the house so he could have some time alone to rest. I instructed Judah to stay on the deck beyond the open sliding glass wall that bordered the kitchen. At the time, a chef was in the throes of preparing food for a dinner party that evening, and all kinds of delightful aromas were wafting through the open expanse and onto the deck where Judah patiently waited for my return.

Once back from our outing, I met my client's son. She had hinted that her son might be a bit of an obstacle in the training process because he was strongly inclined toward doggie treats, but I didn't think much about that until after dinner. I then learned that while we were gone for our one-hour training walk, the lady's son had attempted to bribe my dog with food to enter the kitchen. I was very proud to hear that not only did my trusty Judah not accept any of the food the young man offered, my dog refused to set foot in the house.

Despite my prolonged absence, having left Judah in a strange environment in the midst of strangers while being exposed to the savory smells of cooking, my dog upheld all the dictums of his training and denied himself the forbidden temptations. This is a simple yet profound illustration of what it means to have a well-trained, self-governing dog.

CHAPTER 10

Our minds can shape the way a thing will be because we act accordingly to our expectations. Fredrico Fellini

Raising the Expectation Bar

MOST PEOPLE ARE quick to agree that a responsible dog owner considers training as a top priority, but few fully grasp what *effective* training involves. If you want to take your dog to a level of self-governance similar to what I achieved with Judah, Esther, and my other dogs, you need to first set some specific goals and practice visualization. You need to imagine what the end result of your training efforts will look like. Let me emphasize that this is not only possible but it is essential to your dog's quality of life. When you can give your dog off-leash freedom in a variety of unfamiliar, distracting environments without incurring any embarrassing mishaps, accidents, or emergencies, you will have achieved the ultimate test of your leadership. That's how I define training success.

If today, you were to take the leash off your dog and tell him to lie down and stay, would your pet obey those commands despite the presence of other dogs, people, or small wild critters? If you were out of your dog's line of sight, would he or she "stay" until you return, despite the multitude of temptations or distractions that abound? In short, is your dog trained to that level of self-governance?

When asked these questions, most dog owners sheepishly shake their heads, but I assure them that it isn't entirely their fault. More than once in this book, I outline the ineffectiveness of a positive reinforcement approach to dog training and the folly of common myths such as "You can't expect much from a puppy" or "That's just the nature of the breed." Dog owners around the globe have unwittingly set low performance standards because modern training methods and the average obedience classes are so lacking in accountability, discipline, and consequences. Frustrated owners tolerate all kinds of misbehaviors because they've been trained to *expect* them. But it doesn't have to be this way.

For example, commanding your dog to "stay" means he will stay until you give the release command. This doesn't mean your dog waits thirty seconds and then sets itself free. A dog that will stay put for an hour, despite all temptations, is a dog that can be trusted. This is a self-governing dog that knows how to stay safe—one that will ultimately be rewarded with the freedom of enjoying life to the fullest. Conversely, a dog that falls short of this level is destined for a frustrating life filled with mixed messages, arbitrary restrictions, and possible harm.

If your dog has failed obedience classes, let me rescue you from feeling let down by your canine pal. *Your dog did not fail its training; the training failed your dog.* Many of my clients, most of whom took their dogs through various kinds of obedience classes before working with me, report nightmare stories of what it felt like to flunk the course. Some owners whose dogs just didn't measure up were relegated to a distant corner, isolated from the rest of the group. They were shunned and ignored because their dogs had "issues." A few were even asked not to come back because their dogs were considered too much of a disruption. Excuse me, but wasn't that the reason for attending the obedience classes in the first place—to correct behavioral problems?

Humble Beginnings

Contrary to what my clients often assume, my childhood experience with dogs was less than exceptional. Both of our family dogs fell miserably short of the performance bar I now help my clients reach. Our first dog was a beagle named Ruffy who ran out of our front door one day and was nowhere to be found. After driving all over the neighborhood, my dad finally found Ruffy and brought him home, bloody and writhing in pain. It was obvious he'd been run over. Dad put our injured dog in the car and drove off, and we never saw Ruffy again. I was maybe four at the time, but I still remember the trauma. Too many of us have similar stories from our childhoods, but what did people know about dog ownership in those days?

When I was ten and eager to try again, my sister and I begged our parents for another dog. They finally relented, but Dad chose the breed. He had always wanted a German shepherd, so that's what we got. As with many families, before our parents said we could have a dog, my sister and I faithfully promised to clean up after our pet.

We brought our puppy home and I took "Major" to the basement so he could sniff around and get familiar with his new surroundings. I was soon offered my first chance to make good on my fervent promise of cleanup detail. The pup walked under the staircase and made a deposit that literally had to be half his size! Dad looked at me with a smirk and said, "There you go, son. That's your job!" Oddly enough, I don't recall my sister ever actually cleaning up any dog poop. I think she must have been busy that decade.

A Major Lesson

With predictable youthful enthusiasm, I was keen to teach Major some tricks. With the help of my trusty box of Milk-Bones, I patiently told the dog to "sit" while placing him in the desired position. Each time I did this, I would give him a dog treat. He seemed distracted and scatterbrained, but after maybe half an hour, when I gave the command to "sit," he sat. Instant success; I couldn't believe it! I ran through the house screaming, "He sat! He sat!" I was over the top. This was a victory of enormous proportion; our new dog was smart! We had won the canine brain lottery—we weren't one of those unfortunate families that get stuck with a dumb dog.

Throughout Major's life, we rewarded him with treats after asking him to sit. It went without question that you must always ask a dog to sit before handing him a goodie. Someone, somewhere, in the annals of human history, had arrived at this critical conclusion and passed it down through the generations. Who were we to question this ancient wisdom? Future societies might suffer untold horrors if we should be so cavalier as to break this time-honored tradition of liberally dispensing dog biscuits!

A Not-So-Perfect Dog®

Despite my initial jubilation over Major's apparent intelligence, and despite his seeming obedience in responding to my food rewards, he quickly became a thorn in our sides. We were a typical family that unquestioningly accepted the traditional practice of dog ownership. Like everyone around us, we fell prey to the generally accepted low standards of what it meant to have a family dog. Obedience meant that your dog didn't bite the kids and sometimes your pet did what you wanted; other times you weren't quite so lucky. Our passive acceptance of more-or-less obedience failed us, and it failed our dog miserably when it came to facing the distractions and routines of real life.

But it's not like we didn't try. Dad had taken Major through two consecutive eight-week training courses from which Major graduated with flying colors. This term was proudly bandied about at the time, implying that the training was over and we would all live happily ever after. But that wasn't the case. My dad could never solve Major's aggression problem as it worsened through the years. There were other issues too. Our dog was a profound leash puller, and he never held a stay command for longer than he wanted to. He bolted out the gate when it was left open, jumped on people, harassed our guests, and refused to retrieve. Does any of this sound familiar?

A Major Problem

So training our dog wasn't really what you could call a rousing success. But over the next few years, Major trained *us* to do a lot of tricks. For example, we learned that whining meant we needed to let him out, and barking at the door meant it was time to let him in. When he was bored and pent up with energy, which was often, we'd be opening and closing the door every five minutes! You might say we all passed *our* training with flying colors.

Major had little contact with the world beyond our fenced yard except for two short daily walks on the leash with Dad because he was the only person in the family strong enough to deal with the pulling. I had long ago given up trying to walk Major on my own. There were times my parents would send me out into the yard to play with the dog (meaning they wanted both of us out of their hair), but by now, I was pretty disenchanted with our pet. My playtime with Major was unsatisfying and typically short-lived.

Instead of playing fetch like I wanted, he would run away with the ball until I was so mad I'd storm back into the house, grumbling "Stupid dog!" Major may have passed his eight weeks of training without a hitch, but he couldn't do the simplest thing like return a ball! This meant we couldn't play a game that would have given him the attention and exercise he wanted and needed. I had dreamed of owning a smart dog, but I concluded that ours was so dumb he couldn't even figure out how to fetch. To make matters worse, I was still the one responsible for cleaning up after him, which was almost a full-time job!

Intelligence Is Overrated, Good Training Isn't

Just as I thought our dog Major was missing some smarts, our society as a whole still believes it's possible to bring home a "dumb" dog. When it comes to picking out a new puppy, would-be owners cling to the fervent hope that their pet will be smart. But when people ask me which breeds are the most intelligent (and they often do), I like to say that all dogs possess the requisite intelligence to respond to my *Perfect Dog®* instruction. I explain that while some breeds might be more adept at problem solving than others, this capability has *no* effect on how responsive a dog will be to its owners during and after its training.

Within the same litter of puppies, levels of intelligence will vary, but this doesn't mean any of the pups are incapable of fully understanding what you want from them. Differences in personality and strength of will have a bearing on how *easy* it is to train one dog compared to another, but these factors don't necessarily determine the final results of your training efforts. Some of the most difficult puppies can grow into the greatest of dogs once their headstrong tendencies are effectively harnessed; my once-aggressive dogs Esther and Judah are prime examples.

The training principles and boundaries we teach our dogs don't really require elevated levels of brilliance or problem solving. Effective training involves simple commands, with the expectation that the dog will perform obediently and consistently under varying levels of distraction. Your goal as an owner should be to have your dog respond to *all* of your instructions— every time, under all circumstances, no questions asked.

For instance, every dog on the planet is capable of coming back to its owner's side when off leash, despite any distraction. And every dog is capable of holding an extended "down, stay" in real-life situations, off the leash and even out of the owner's sight. This means you don't have to get caught up in searching for the smartest breed because even a so-called dumb dog can perform at the same level as a so-called smart one. What makes the critical difference is the effectiveness of the training: the secret of maximizing a dog's true potential is *training* power, not brainpower.

Believe it or not, I have met people who have taken their dog to the veterinarian for hearing tests because their pet didn't respond to repeated calls from a distance. No matter how loud or long the owners yelled, their dogs would take no notice. While no hearing deficiencies were diagnosed, the owners still found it difficult to accept that the deafness was selective. In other words, the dogs didn't have any kind of physical affliction; they ignored their owners because they suffered from a condition called poor training.

The Road Less Traveled

When it comes to opening our eyes to the possibilities of effective dog training, a simple turn of mind can do a lot of good. The willingness to move away from traditional ways of thinking can help dogs and their owners achieve a fulfilling relationship and the life of freedom they deserve. Once we realize that age, breed, size, gender, intelligence level, or even history doesn't limit a dog's training potential, we will have broken new ground.

We can unlearn the long-established myths and commonly held erroneous beliefs and begin relearning new ways of perceiving the dog's true potential and working toward it. We can embrace new training approaches that actually work. With this newly gained wisdom, we can consciously set our goals and then seek the knowledge and skills that will help us achieve our vision. We can turn our back on the dysfunctional thinking that does nothing but keep us stuck in a mind-set fraught with limitations.

If this sounds lofty, it is. But the best part is that it's doable. We can't rewrite history, but we can leave it behind. We can establish new ground rules for the relationships we share with our dogs. We can create a new way of thinking and being that results in a bond brimming with harmony, freedom, and joy. Why would anyone want to settle for anything less?

CHAPTER 11

Self-confidence is the first requisite to great undertakings. —Samuel Johnson

In retrospect, achieving his childhood dream didn't seem quite as appealing as he had imagined.

And a Child Shall Lead Them

MY TWO YOUNG sons have worked with me around dogs since they were old enough to walk. Despite their tender years, they both have a solid understanding of what it takes to get a dog to obey them because both of my boys have been taught the proper way to gain instant respect from dogs. I have seen my sons approached by large, rambunctious dogs that habitually disrespect their owners. These dogs have bounded up to my children, ready to bully or dominer, only to be instantly humbled. It's entertaining to see the look on a dog's face and the manners it suddenly discovers when confronted by two young boys who refuse to be intimidated. My sons can then freely move around the dog without fear of being jumped on, knocked over, or having their snacks stolen.

As one of my clients arrived for our first session, I watched her dog determinedly drag her across our parking area. I took the leash and, after a brief explanation, began working with her dog. I soon passed the pooch off to my oldest son who was only four years old at the time. This dog was as big as my boy, but Ethan confidently and competently walked the dog on a loose leash. He then dropped the leash, giving the dog a firm "down" command followed by a firm "stay" command.

My son then walked in a large circle around the dog before coming back to stand beside the dog without patting him. Ethan picked up the leash, paused, and then clapped his hands, giving the "okay" release command. The dog stood up, and my boy rewarded him with physical and verbal praise, the dog looking completely satisfied with this simple prize from his new little leader.

The owner was stunned that such a young boy was able to get her boisterous dog to behave so obediently when only moments before she had been "leash skiing" across our driveway. And yes, I was very proud of my son! This story illustrates that from a pack hierarchy perception, it only takes a dog a few seconds to size up whether he is dealing with a human leader or follower. I believe that when children are trained from the time they are tiny and empowered with the proper methods, they have the capability to handle a dog with mastery. Even a small child, through body language and tone of voice, can communicate leadership in a human-canine relationship.

Kids and Dogs

Unfortunately, the average child has not been privileged with the same kind of exposure to 24/7 dog training as my sons have. There still exists an age-old problem between kids and dogs whereby most children handle dogs with fairytale expectations, and this predicament can have grave ramifications. I encourage everyone to aim high when it comes to visualizing training goals, and while it's great that a child hopes for the best with his dog, the problem is that most kids lack a realistic view of what can be achieved.

Think back on your own childhood and recall the classic Hollywood portrayals of dogs and how these depictions shaped your concept of the relationship you wanted with your pet. These conjured images must be put into perspective before kids can realistically and effectively relate to their family dogs. My own story demonstrates how ill equipped youngsters can be when visions of Lassie dance in their heads, and there's no realistic training program to balance things out. Perhaps you have a similar story in your history.

The Confidence Factor

Clients often press me to let their children play a major role in their dog's initial training. The few times I've given in to this pressure, I have more often than not regretted my decision because it's extremely difficult trying to work with children or teens who are wrestling with self-esteem issues. I get the feeling that this is the first time in their lives these kids have been put in a position of such responsibility, and although this could be a great learning experience for them, they sorely lack the skills for rising to the task.

Training a dog requires self-confidence and presence of mind. For various reasons, most children today simply do not have the resolve to ride through the short-term challenges that yield long-term success. For example, instead of making firm, effective corrections, a youngster might back down at the very first sign of protest from their dog, reinforcing rebellion instead of overriding it.

Meanwhile, either the child's enabling parents step in and take over the disciplinary role, or they sabotage the effort with suggestions of compromise. Instead of being educated about the importance of accountability, discipline, and consequence (excellent concepts that apply to many facets of life), the child is encouraged to give up. The message is "You are ineffective." Self-esteem takes another nosedive. I've determined not to venture onto this minefield again, despite parental assurance that everyone is qualified for the job.

Granted, I've had a few encouraging experiences along the way, but the children I've successfully worked with have been more mature than their peers; they've been raised to be responsible and pragmatic. Because these positive experiences have been the minority, I now recommend that parents first establish a foundation for the training. Once the owners have gained the dog's respect and obedience, their children can start working with the dog—closely supervised at first so correct technique can be applied and self-confidence can grow. By this time, the owners have overcome the dog's initial defiance or resistance, and the children can now get involved at an appropriate level and pace.

This doesn't mean I'm against the whole "kids and dogs" thing. Certainly, if you truly believe your child has the requisite skills to contribute to your dog's social development, then grant him or her the awesome challenge of being involved from the beginning. Just make sure you're actively overseeing the process. Your child will benefit mightily from the experience.

As I state above, my opinion about kids training dogs is based on experience. By nature I am a realist and, because of my profession, my heart lies with what is best for the dog. In short, it's unfair to subject a dog to the inconsistencies of an insecure, inexperienced child's murky commands. It's also unfair to place too much responsibility on a youngster; the chance of success is far less than the inevitability of problems for both parties down the road.

The Value of a Life

When parents leave the dog's training *solely* on a child, their intent is honorable. They want to teach their kid responsibility, but you would probably agree that this is some extremely hefty delegation. I liken it to letting a neighbor rebuild the transmission on your Ferrari because he has a few tools on hand and thinks he can do it. When it comes to car repair, we make sure our vehicle is in the right hands, yet our dog and child are of priceless value compared to a physical possession. When a dog's quality of life or our child's self-esteem might be in question, it makes great sense to keep our priorities in order.

Simply put, when unskilled children are left in charge of training the family dog, there's a huge factor to consider: safety. If children don't know how to effectively discipline the dog, there exists the possibility of unpleasant to downright dangerous consequences—if not to the dog, then to the child. Because most kids lack sufficient knowledge, experience, and understanding about how the dog's mind works, they can be easy targets for abuse from a dog, or vice versa. Please believe me; the outcomes have the potential of breaking your heart.

A Dire Deed

One such grim incident happened in the United States. A six-year-old girl was playing in her backyard. It was a cold, blustery day, so the girl was bundled up in her winter clothes with a long scarf around her neck to keep out the wind. The mother let the dog out in the yard with her daughter, as she had done many times before. This young and boisterous dog was in the habit of jumping on the girl and tugging at her clothes. The family figured this kind of mischief was normal for a young dog, and he'd eventually grow out of it. No one would ever have imagined what was about to happen.

Once outside, the dog, full of energy, began jumping up and grabbing at the girl's scarf. I speculate that the parents had probably instructed the child (as most parents do) never to hurt the family pet. As the dog continued his playful antics, he would have followed his canine instincts to escalate his advances because of the little girl's subservience to his aggression. Imagine the confusion this child must have experienced, trying to fend away the dog's advances, yet wanting to be a good girl by not being mean to him. The dog's abuse intensified, but the howling wind muted the child's screams. The mother never heard her daughter's impassioned cries for help. The little girl died, strangled by her scarf as the dog dragged her, helpless and struggling, around the yard.

This was a sickening, senseless, needless death with massive undertones. This harrowing story is a grim reminder that seemingly small misbehaviors can sometimes lead to massive disaster.

Tragedies such as these reaffirm my commitment to educate, enlighten, and lead the way toward a level of dog ownership that reaches new heights of companionship, freedom, and safety. Imagine for a moment how much better it would be if such deep, dreadful losses were never, ever to happen again—especially to an innocent child. And that's why I keep doing what I do, because I know there's a better way. And now you know it too.

CHAPTER 12

The obscure we see eventually. The completely obvious takes longer. —Edwin Newman

The Aggression Epidemic

THERE ARE MORE than 4.7 million reported dog bites in the U.S. annually, and over one-sixth of those bites require medical attention. Every hour, forty-four people are admitted to hospital emergency rooms across the United States because of dog bites. Beyond these alarming statistics, consider the millions of attacks that are never reported. If you have some awareness of the dog aggression statistics, perhaps you've wondered if there are genetic issues at play or if this is simply one of those unavoidable social issues we just have to accept as a cost of having pets. Well, hold onto your seat because this is where I really take off.

The topic of dog aggression always stirs me up, and tragedies such as the child strangled by the family dog in her backyard cuts me to the quick. The dog didn't set out to murder the little girl, but its uncorrected aggression resulted in disaster. While such extreme situations are a rarity, they shouldn't ever happen at all. Uncurbed canine dominance can lead to all kinds of painful, bloody calamities where victims are killed or left physically and emotionally scarred for life.

Most people are unaware that when a new puppy enters their home, this little mutt's mother has already instilled a good deal of training in her offspring. If owners could learn and accept this simple but powerful truth, they would approach their puppy's training with corrections that complement the foundation established by the mother dog.

People could build on those early lessons and end up with a respectful, obedient pup (thus ensuring the safety of others) in a surprisingly short period of time. As I write this, yet another newsflash of a child being mauled to death by the family dog has appeared on the Internet. I wonder if she'd still be alive if her parents had known how critical it was to moderate their dog's will when it was yet a seemingly innocent, cute little puppy.

Can You Read the Signs?

Years may pass before a dog's domineering behavior comes to a heartbreaking head. Many owners dismiss the signs, mistaking aggression for minor misbehaviors. Few owners realize that a succession of uncorrected subtle acts of dominance reinforce the dog's notion that he's the pack leader, eventually leading to that first bite, attack, or mauling. Every time the dog snarls when a family member nears its food or toys, every time the dog chases off the postman, and yes, every time the dog is permitted to bully little tykes or tug on their clothes, the animal gains confidence that he is the alpha. And alpha dogs perceive that it's their right to put subordinate pack members in their place any time there's a need.

Simply put, when a dog expresses aggression (a throaty growl, a threatening bark, forceful body language, etc.) upon a canine or human pack member, he is upholding his position of authority. Whether the dog perceives that his leadership is being challenged or he wants his subordinates to behave a certain way, he enforces the rules through dominance. The dog is simply saying, "Back off, pal. I'm boss around here, and I don't like what's happening. Stop it now!"

Most people back off when confronted with aggressive canine behavior, and this usually satisfies the dog, at least for the time being. But when a situation isn't satisfactorily resolved in the dog's mind, the dog may escalate his dominance to the point where someone gets hurt. In the dog's mind, he isn't doing anything wrong; he's simply operating on his pack instincts, raising the stakes, and fulfilling the role he's been allowed to take on.

Acts of rough play (such as wrestling or playing tug of war) are a form of communication between pack members. If you watch a litter of puppies, you will notice their playful romps, chases, and mouthing games. These behaviors are not just mindless entertainment. The puppies are purposely testing one another to see who's the toughest. They are sorting out the pecking order, and the pack hierarchy ranks will be reinforced as they grow up.

There's nothing wrong with playing with your dog, but if you allow your dog to always win or dictate the intensity of the game, you are setting a potentially dangerous precedent. Put simply, if you consistently choose to take a submissive or subordinate role during play, your inferior position will creep into other areas of your relationship with your dog. So the message is to be careful; you could unwittingly promote aggressive inclinations in your canine pal.

When I now flash back to our family dog Major and his uncorrected aggressive tendencies, I can't help but cringe. I still remember how our feisty shepherd would tear envelopes out of the mail slot as the postman dropped our post in the door. I recall the turmoil that ensued every time the doorbell rang. Our dog would bark and jump at the window in the door to show the person on the other side that Major was in charge of our household. We would have to grab our aggressive dog by the collar and drag him into the sewing room where he would be confined until he calmed down.

Later, we would let him out so he could "visit" with the guests. We would tell our friends to stand still and quiet as Major scurried up to them for a once-over. As our visitors stood stiffly in place, we'd tutor them on the getting-acquainted protocol. "Let him sniff you," was always our first instruction. "Once he gets to know you, he's great," we'd add with hopeful encouragement. Like many other owners of dogs with a propensity for dominance, the signs were all there. But in those days, who had the presence of mind to identify aggression for what it really was? The sad part is that this still goes on, in far too many households. We must identify aggression for what it is and not pretend it's just a personality quirk!

Out of the Blue

The next time you watch or read a news story about a dreadful dog attack, pay attention to what the owners have to say. I can almost guarantee that you will hear, "Oh, but he's a wonderful dog, and he's never done anything like this before. It happened completely out of the blue." I can't tell you how many times I've heard statements like this, and maybe you have too. They are said with wholehearted conviction, but what lies beneath those fateful words is denial, pure and simple. To me, this is intolerable.

Most people who own dogs that have attacked seem to believe there were forces at play beyond their control. Provocation on the part of the victim is the most common excuse. These owners go to great lengths in explaining that their dogs are never aggressive at home, and they are eager to regale you with warmhearted stories and lovely moments spent with their "wonderful" pets.

As with other aspects of dog ownership, it's clear to me that when it comes to aggression, emotional investment obscures the ugly truth. Traditional societal filters, labels, and projection of human characteristics onto pets prevent owners from identifying and correcting aggression problems when they first begin. For example, if we've been told from childhood to believe that dogs always bark at strangers and canines are naturally protective of their food—when these things happen, we won't bat an eye.

Knowledge Is Power

Because most people don't understand the nature of dog aggression and what it looks or sounds like, they won't recognize it. Nor will they know how to stop it. As a result, we have a society that is battling what I consider an aggression epidemic, while governments and self-proclaimed experts are using ineffective measures and methods that don't even come close to fixing the problem. Out of desperation (or to keep up appearances), leash laws are tightened, the media promotes that vague concept of "responsible dog ownership," and the public cries out for banning certain breeds. Yet the best, most viable tactic against dog aggression is *prevention*, and that requires a solid understanding of how dogs think—that is, using the dynamics of dog pack hierarchy to discipline and train.

For most people, the words "dog aggression" conjure images of a crazed, vicious beast, fangs bared, ready to pounce and maul an unsuspecting victim. They don't visualize a tiny family pet growling over its dish or a barking puppy that can't be silenced. Until we correctly identify and understand the various expressions of aggression, we will continue being incapable of dealing with the problem head-on.

I yearn for people to realize that it's not cute when a ten-week-old puppy growls over his toy or food dish. This is aggressive behavior, and the dominance must be controlled through the owner's leadership. If this doesn't happen, the pup may grow up to be a danger to his owner family and society at large. The six-year-old girl killed by the family dog would never have been strangled to death if her parents had recognized and subdued their pet's early signs of aggression.

This subject is not about big dogs versus little dogs, nor is it about specific breeds. You might be surprised to learn that the golden retriever once topped the "most wanted" list for dog bites in North America. You might be shocked to know that a Pomeranian once mauled a newborn baby to death; the tiny dog was alone with the infant for only a few minutes while the babysitter was in the kitchen heating the baby's bottle.

Regardless of the size or breed, and regardless of the nature of a dog's aggressive act, the root of the problem can always be traced back to a single cause: ignorance of, and leniency toward, signs of dominance beginning from the day the pup was brought home. Once this common causal factor becomes clearly understood, the solution is the same for all owners. Wake up, drop the denial, curb your emotions, swallow your pride, admit that your dog is showing signs of aggressiveness, and start a consistent training program based on accountability, discipline, and consequences.

We Need to Walk Our Talk

I was once asked to appear on a TV discussion forum about dog attacks. A runaway family dog had recently savaged a blind man's guide dog, and the community was seeking expert advice from dog professionals on how to prevent such incidents in the future. I was the only panel member who didn't invoke the predictable, vague, and politically correct suggestion of "responsible dog ownership." One of the guests (a new-age-type dog trainer) was openly resistant to my pragmatic suggestions.

After the show aired, I learned an interesting piece of information about this woman. She owned two dogs, one of which she took everywhere she went and the other she kept under close tabs because of its embarrassing and dangerous aggressive tendencies. I was told that she was at her wit's end and ready to have this dog euthanized.

Though she proclaimed herself a trainer, the woman had only tried corrective methods that fell within her realm of emotional comfort such as confinement or limiting the dog's exposure to situations that might set him off. Obviously, none of her tactics had worked on her unruly pet. There *must* be more to controlling aggression than cleverly avoiding circumstances where a dog might display its dangerous dominance, because avoidance techniques simply treat the symptom, not the cause.

If the woman had stifled her stubbornness and been open to my advice the day of the forum, life with her dog could have taken a different path. I never found out what happened in the end, but that confidential information made me wonder if yet another poor dog needlessly lost its life because of human pride and shortsightedness.

Tip the Scale in Your Favor

Every aggressive dog has a point at which it will realize that it's no longer worth trying to be in command of the pack. It's your job to simply tough it out, consistently showing your pet in no uncertain terms that you will not tolerate his behavior. During this period of adjustment, fortify the discipline with deserved praise, affection, and play whenever you notice that your dog is responding positively to the changing relationship. It's a battle of wills, and you must be the victor. You want peace of mind. You want safety for yourself and your family, and anyone else who comes into contact with your dog. The risk of any other outcome is absolutely not worth it.

When you start training a dog, the moment your disciplinary measures match the level of your pet's self-perceived ranking in the pack, he starts to feel threatened. Of course, low-ranking dogs tend to relinquish their authority more readily than more aggressive canines. But the "top dogs" can be alarmingly stubborn. They will expend their entire arsenal in their efforts to force you into submission. You must stand your ground.

Don't be tricked into thinking that your dog doesn't understand. If you communicate even halfway clearly, your dog will comprehend what you're asking. And here's what you must understand: you need to place—and keep—yourself at the top of the hierarchy, or your dog won't revere you enough to *always* obey your commands. When you emerge as the new consistent leader, the battle of wills is over and you have earned your dog's respect.

On the other hand, if you relent and end up in the subordinate position, you have a lifetime of trouble waiting in the wings. I describe more than once in this book the disobedient, destructive, and dangerous behaviors perpetrated by dogs that think they're running the show. This is the road to continual frustration and disillusionment, or worse. To establish yourself as the leader, your discipline and corrections must be consistent every time your dog challenges your authority.

When I use the word *consistent*, I mean communicating in an absolute, undeviating pattern, clearly conveying beyond all doubt that you are the one in charge. You don't backpedal or relent out of guilt or laziness. You don't lapse into moments of lenience, make excuses, or allow exceptions out of misplaced compassion because those are the exact ways you lose your pet's respect. Aggressive dogs—regardless of size or age—aim for the peak of the pack's hierarchy, and unless your persistence and consistency outlast and eclipse your dog's determination to lead, you risk losing the top spot. This is, of course, something you simply cannot afford to do.

Success Is Achieved a Step at a Time

Occasionally, my *Perfect Dog®* training system has been blamed for making a dog aggressive; this is an incorrect assumption. In reality, my method was responsible for *exposing* the dog's true nature. Understanding a pet's temperament is the first step in building a leader-subordinate relationship, and it marks the beginning of positive change, but only if the owner follows through.

My system offers both the tools and the step-by-step instructions to help a dog make the critical mental shift that enables it to deal more constructively with problematic situations. But first, you need to know exactly what kind of canine personality you're dealing with so you know what level to work at. You can be consistent in your training efforts with unwavering diligence, but *unless you communicate at a level greater than your dog's self-perceived ranking on the pack hierarchy scale, he will never learn to respect you as his superior.*

Although your dog's resistance to your initial training efforts may feel uncomfortable, it's an opportunity for you to pave a new pathway for him to follow. For instance, you can teach your dog that instead of going nuts every time a stranger walks by the bay window, he needs to remain calm and defer to you as leader. That is, instead of your dog barking to enforce *his* domain, train him to depend on you to make the call about how the situation should be handled.

Too many owners throw in the towel too early in the face-off between themselves and their aggressive dogs. By taking just a few more steps or persisting for a few more hours or days, you will achieve success. Climbing a mountain requires having a vision and taking one step at a time—over and over and over again. It takes courage and perseverance to continue taking those steps when parts of you are tired and begging to quit. But once you reach the summit, the scenery is expansive and breathtaking. The panorama plus your feelings of accomplishment are the rewards for your hard work. The same applies to the heights you can reach with your dog if you're willing to take one step at a time until you achieve your goal.

Hold on to the Vision

Aggression is one of the most common justifications for pet euthanization, but rarely is this problem unsolvable. If you have an aggressive dog, you need to visualize peace and safety for all as you match wills with your pet. Let this image of success inspire you through the tough times and give you the grit to keep on going. And to be realistic, you also need to seriously consider the possible consequences of not achieving your goal.

On rare occasions, a dog might remain unpredictable and unreliable even after thorough, proper training; its psychological instability might render it incapable of change. Other times, when dogs are specifically bred and trained for aggression (such as the horrific illegal dog-fighting operations that exist in the dark recesses of this world), even the best of trainings cannot completely undo the damage. But those cases are isolated and uncommon.

Let me state again that the average aggressive dog should not have to lose his life because his owners have failed to rise above their denial, emotions, or societal pressures. Making excuses, justifying, and coddling a dominant dog fans the flames of aggression. I can't stand the thought of people killing their dogs while claiming they "did everything they possibly could, but nothing worked."

Consider that aggression issues never go unresolved in a dog pack. The leader either successfully contains subordinate uprisings to maintain group harmony, or he is challenged and overcome by a younger and stronger successor. As a caring, competent owner, you have an advantage: while repeated confrontations with your strong-willed dog may make you feel tired, wired, or frayed at the edges, you have intelligence, mental hardiness, and fortitude on your side. Apply these qualities wisely and generously, and you will potentially save your dog's life. It is infinitely rewarding for me to see peace and calm in the eyes of a once-aggressive dog. He seems to say, "Thank you for taking on the burden of leadership. It is the most valuable gift you could have ever given me."

Not So Far-Fetched

When Gary Larsen's *Far Side* comic strip came on the scene, I was captivated by his humor. My favorite Larsen cartoon depicts an older couple welcoming two friends for dinner. As the hosts stand at the open door flanked by their large, scruffy, intimidating dog, they greet their guests by name and then say, "Now quickly, place one hand across your throat and the other hand confidently on top of Bruno's head. This darned dog is going to get us into a major lawsuit one day!"

I laughed aloud when I read the caption. This cartoon perfectly portrayed the plight of owners who have not properly trained their aggressive dogs; it certainly reminded me of the problems we had with our dog Major. Humor aside, too many owners adapt to their aggressive dogs instead of insisting that the dogs conform to their standards. These frustrated, browbeat people are destined to live in an uneasy and tenuous state, constantly holding their breath, keeping their fingers crossed, and hoping for a happy ending.

But a happy ending can't occur when the work hasn't been done, and this is where the laughing stops. The dog lives an anxious and pitiful existence. The owners fare much the same. One day someone gets seriously threatened, hurt, and in some cases, even killed. By then, the owners have little recourse but to take the dog's life in response.

If we truly love our dogs, we will do what it takes to train our pets so they will respect us and obey us. In exchange, our pets get to live full and happy lives, free from the potential menace of aggression. We can't let excuses derail our goal of a mutually rewarding relationship, and we can't allow emotions or social pressures to weaken our resolve.

Most of all, we can't give up. What we can do instead is doggedly hang on to our vision of the future and work toward it every day, in every single interaction with our dogs. This way, we can reach our personal summit step by step. Everyone around us will repeatedly reap the benefits of our journey: freedom, companionship, and quality of life for all concerned. The rewards are there for the taking, and it's certainly worth the trek.

CHAPTER 13

No one means all he says, and yet very few say all they mean, for words are slippery and thought is viscous. —Henry Adams

The moral dilemma of a mailman's dog.

The Trouble with Labels

MORE THAN ONCE in this book, I mention undefined words (labels) that fly from people's mouths so freely and casually. Labels or stereotypical words may sound impressive, legitimate, and even profound, yet they can deceive the listener. This is because labels and mental constructs are based on generalized assumptions and not specific definitions. Take the term "responsible dog owner" for example. This phrase is commonly used as a panacea for just about any dog problem that exists (and I'll admit I use it a few times in this book), but I *define* what it means in behavioral terms. Here's the problem with generalized statements: what does "responsible dog owner" mean? Your definition may differ from mine; in fact, it probably does! Words can be fuzzy.

A responsible dog owner could be interpreted as a person who walks his dog twice a day, keeps his dog on a leash at all times when outdoors, provides sufficient healthy food for his pet, and takes his dog to the vet for regular checkups. But by now, you know that what I mean by responsible dog ownership runs much deeper than that. It's that 24/7 lifelong training program that helps the dog develop into the most self-governing, well-adjusted, well-behaved animal it can be.

All words have meanings to all people, of course, but not all interpretations of a word's meaning are the same. There's the dictionary definition, or *denotative* meaning, also known as the formal definition. But labels play off the *connotative* meaning of words—that is, an individual's personal, subjective definition of what it means. Connotative meaning involves emotions and perceptions because it's *our* definition, not one that's listed in a book. And when we operate from perception instead of fact or reality, we risk misunderstanding or being misled. We may lower our standards and accept a less-than-ideal situation without realizing that better choices exist. This is how some people who may otherwise be intelligent, educated, and logical in other areas of their lives tolerate and excuse some of the most outrageous misbehaviors in their dogs. I present many examples in this book.

You have probably had times in your life when words got you into trouble with someone you care about. On the other hand, it was probably words that helped clear up the situation too. In essence, language influences perceptions. Because words can be used to masterfully influence, persuade, or outright manipulate, owners need to be cautioned about the various labels bandied about by professionals in the dog industry. Some trainers intentionally play on emotion with the use of euphemisms or fuzzy phrases instead of "telling it like it is." Impressionable dog owners, swayed by evocative labels and the mental images they conjure, choose emotion over logic. This is why so many well-meaning owners buy into the lenient positive-reinforcement (food) training approach. It *sounds* so good for the owner and tastes so good for the dog.

Three common phrases an owner might hear are *fear aggression, separation anxiety,* and *rescue dog.* Forbearance is shown toward the fear-aggressive dog because it appears to be in a prolonged state of emotional distress. As for separation anxiety, owners often go to great lengths to accommodate their pet because of its apparent forlorn nature and needy personality. And the maladjusted rescue dog ends up being overindulged because of its (assumed) abusive past.

The continual use of emotion-laden humanistic terms seduces owners into thinking they're obligated to cosset their dogs. Sadly, when bad behaviors are tolerated or accepted instead of being effectively corrected, both dog and owner are condemned to a life of frustration, mixed emotions, or worse. People can only handle chaos for so long, and then they resort to desperate measures.

Even the most tolerant dog owners have a breaking point. After too many months or years of trying to live with an extreme, untenable situation, these owners believe there's only one drastic option left: having their dogs euthanized. Few people want to think about—let alone discuss—this grim subject, and the figures are shocking. In the U.S. alone, the Humane Society estimates that animal shelters care for six to eight million dogs and cats every year, with approximately half of these animals being euthanized because they are unfit for adoption. Keep in mind that these staggering numbers are estimates because there is no central reporting agency for animal shelters. But even if the figures were only half these amounts, this is still a disturbing, alarming statistic.

Additionally, these estimates *do not* include the animals euthanized in private veterinary hospitals because of behavioral problems. Using the Humane Society's annual estimate of up to four million deaths, this equates to 76,923 per week—or 10,989 animals terminated every day, with nearly eight pets dying every minute. Forgive me for being so graphic, but here's the point: if people were educated about the causes and effects of dog misbehavior, and if they employed a training method that yields actual results, the sickening number of needless pet deaths could be substantially reduced.

Distinguishing between Symptoms and the Cause

It may come as no surprise to you that the most common reasons people have their dogs euthanized are connected to aggression, separation anxiety, and unmanageability (a series of extreme misbehaviors linked to overpampering, leniency, and grossly inconsistent discipline). Many owners and professionals alike simply don't know how to permanently cure these behavioral issues. Once again, this demonstrates the danger of using labels for symptoms instead of addressing the cause. If more trainers could comprehend why dogs behave as they do, if they based their approach on how dogs think and act from the perspective of pack dynamics—they could effect permanent behavior change. And if owners operated from the *canine* perspective instead of foisting human characteristics upon their charges, the pet death rate would plummet.

Fear Aggression

Although I cover the topic of aggression in the previous chapter, it's important to explain that whether a dog's aggressiveness is rooted in fear or dominion, its physical expression of aggression (whether barking, growling, snarling, or lunging, or a combination of these actions) is unacceptable, and the behaviors must be corrected. Whether a dog is expressing fear or a desire to dominate, it must learn *never* to challenge its owner for the position of leadership regardless of the situation.

Recall the dog's need to know where it fits within the pack hierarchy. For the fearful dog, the pecking order brings security. For the dog with dominant tendencies, it learns self-governance. In dog-human relationships, the pecking order absolutely must be established, or all members of the group will suffer the consequences. Owners who can't understand (or won't accept) this basic concept live in constant fear of being too harsh or too firm, and they continually let their dogs off the hook instead of insisting on obedience. But just as the leader of a dog pack suffers no guilt or self-doubt, owners must be crystal clear and consistent about the issue of leadership and who is in charge.

We must set our emotions aside and rise above sympathy or culpability so we can do what is ultimately best for our pets. A fear-aggressive dog loses out with the soft approach because, without clear boundaries, it will remain emotionally unstable and resort to its natural defenses when forced to cope with uncomfortable situations. Soft-approach trainers and enabling owners unknowingly cause fear-based aggression to become more firmly entrenched in the dog's character, with everyone (including the dog) getting more of what they don't want. Put simply, though it may seem counterintuitive, the fear-aggressive dog wants and needs an owner who will confidently take the reins and remain in charge.

A Roadside Hazard

When I was living in Canada, a woman asked me for help with a large black golden retriever cross she had acquired from a local shelter. It was quickly evident that her dog was fear aggressive, but she didn't call it that. She described her pet as being deathly afraid of parked cars, which made going for walks virtually impossible. By this time in my career, I had worked with many fearful dogs, but I had never heard of one being afraid of parked cars! Perhaps the dog had been hit by a speeding vehicle or had had a dangerously close call, but that was irrelevant. Experience told me that any negative history crippling this dog could be completely overwritten by a new positive mental outlook.

The first two days, I focused on beginning the groundwork (teaching the dog to walk on the leash without pulling, and to obey the "down" and "stay" commands). I must say he exhibited quite a bit of resistance over being told what to do. The third day, the owner—impatient for results—pleaded with me to address the parked-car issue, and we headed down my long driveway toward the road.

At that time, I lived in a somewhat rural area, but there was always the occasional car parked along the roadside. As we neared the end of my driveway, I spotted our first vehicle about fifty feet ahead. When we were about half that distance from the car, the client's dog reared up on his hind legs and began thrashing about, pulling on the leash and snapping his teeth in a violent attempt to retreat. We backed off just far enough for the dog to calm down, and I immediately put a muzzle on him.

About Face

As I expected, the dog's initial reaction to the object he feared was the classic stress-induced "flight or fight" response (common to people as well as animals). But in this case, flight—or running away from the car—was impossible for the dog because I had him on a leash and wasn't about to let go. As I made him walk closer to the car, he resorted to the fight response (aggression). If any bystanders had seen the dog snapping and throwing itself around, they would never have diagnosed the dog as being afraid. He looked—and felt—like a lean, mean fighting machine!

In case you're wondering why I muzzled the dog, I did it for two reasons. First, it would keep me from getting bitten as we closed in on the parked car and the dog began pitching its fit. Second, it would force the dog to accept the reality of the situation: he had to learn that attempting to resolve his distress by becoming aggressive would be futile. I was putting the dog in a situation where his default stress strategies would no longer work. He couldn't flee because of the leash in my hand, and fighting wasn't going to work either because I had disarmed him with the muzzle.

For canines and human beings alike, fear can be a debilitating factor that expands and escalates with every repeated exposure. These episodes are often labeled as panic attacks. But when a fear is finally faced and debunked, we are freed from its hold for the rest of our lives. This was my mission: to help the dog conquer his fears. And once again, we approached the dog's most dreaded and feared object.

My next move was something few people might presume to do. With a firm hand on the dog's collar, I wrestled him right up to the vehicle. Positioning the dog between the car and myself (but not so close he could damage or scratch it), I marched him around and around the vehicle for about twenty minutes. Finally, the dog stopped struggling. He now walked next to me, calmly and quietly, as we took a few more revolutions around the formerly terrifying object.

We then headed farther down the road, marching toward the next parked car. As we neared vehicle number two, the dog's reaction was the same as the first time. He reared up again and, with unchecked vehemence, tried to wrestle away from me. Once more, I grabbed his collar so he could get up close and personal with this second mechanical monster. My work only took half as long this time; in ten minutes, the dog was beginning to realize that I refused to take no for an answer, and that maybe—just maybe—parked cars were not quite as horrendous as he once thought.

Riding the wave of this second victory, I pointed him toward a third parked vehicle. This time, to my client's amazement, her dog and I walked up to the car and around it without the slightest hesitation. Every parked car we passed on the rest of our walk came and went without a blink from this formerly fear-aggressive dog.

You Can't Argue With Results

The owner called me later that evening. With unbridled excitement, she described how she and her husband had taken the dog for a walk that evening with the same wonderful results we had achieved earlier. Case closed! It really didn't matter to me *why* the dog had developed this quirky fear of parked cars; my job was simply to fix it. I didn't need to psychoanalyze him, and I certainly didn't want to sympathize or try to justify his fear. That would have only reinforced the problem.

Some might argue that the dog was traumatized at being forced to get so close to the cars, that it would have been kinder to use a more passive or gentler approach. But I look at it this way: the dog was traumatized by its own fear! I don't think it's too far-fetched to suggest that some trainers might have decorated a line of parked cars with canine cookies for weeks on end, hoping the dog would tackle his metallic demons via his taste buds. But to me, it would have been cruel and inhumane to chance letting fear prevent this poor animal from fully enjoying his life when I knew there was a sure solution. Something had to be done, and now was the time.

In fact, the owner had already tried a number of "kinder, gentler" techniques, and none of them had worked. She hired me to get results. Too much of today's dog training revolves around trying to make the owners emotionally comfortable instead of working from the *dog's* point of view. A firm hand; a brief, repeated disciplinary action; or a stern command may appear strong or seem mean to a bystander, but this is language a dog understands from the moment of its birth. If you ever have the pleasure of watching puppies with their mother, note the short, assertive teaching techniques she uses to get their attention or discipline them, and how quickly her offspring get the message. Oh, that we human beings could be so consistent and effective!

We're all familiar with the phrase: "Fight fire with fire." Why not be direct with dogs because that's how *they* communicate? Why not help dogs learn how to behave properly by speaking their language? By directly addressing the situation, I was able to cure a dramatic, debilitating problem that was traumatizing both a dog and its owner. And it only took half an hour.

Separation Anxiety

What we commonly call canine separation anxiety is in actuality a behavioral problem most often exacerbated by owners projecting human emotions onto their dogs. Calling separation anxiety a condition makes it extremely difficult for owners to correct the misbehavior with discipline. While owners might conclude that their dog with "abandonment issues" is pining or longing for the company of its human pack to the point of suffering in their absence, it's much simpler than that.

The dog with separation anxiety isn't fearful that its owners have deserted or abandoned him. The dog is spoiled, pure and simple. It's being bossy and demanding. The pampered pooch's real message is "How dare you? Come back here! You have no right to leave me, and I'm going to scream and yell and tear up the house in defiance if you don't meet my demands!" Believe it or not, there are desperate dog owners who actually hire "babysitters" for their tantrum-throwing pets so they can leave in peace and return without having to replace clothing or furniture, or hose down every room. To me, this kind of domestic doggie terrorism is completely and absolutely intolerable.

If only these owners grasped that they're unwittingly buying into their dog's anxious behaviors and neurotic tics—if only they understood that they are systematically creating a codependent, dysfunctional relationship! These owners, by submissively catering to their animal's every whim or subtle signal of need, have taught their dogs to be demanding, manipulative, and controlling. The dogs quickly assume the pack leader position once they learn how easy it is to "train" their human beings to meet their every desire. If it weren't so sad, it might be funny. Tragically, too many of these out-of-control dogs end up euthanized because they make life so intolerable for their desperate owners. I regard this situation as pathetic. And once again, may I state that it doesn't have to be this way.

The good news is that this "condition" can turn around surprisingly fast once owners decide to reclaim the leadership role and act like the higher life form. The truth is so simple: *dogs are surprisingly adaptable when social roles are clear.* Most of the time, a dog classified as suffering from separation anxiety will suddenly demonstrate that he can actually cope quite well on his own once it's clear that the owner is now the one running the show.

In explaining both the problem of separation anxiety and its solution in just a few paragraphs, the subject may not seem like much. But left untreated (or worse, unwittingly encouraged), it can result in thousands of dollars of ruined possessions, endless frustration at perpetual paybacks, and even destruction of the canine perpetrator himself. These are huge, unnecessary losses. Potentially serious outcomes are at risk when owners enable their dogs to the nth degree. But just as with overly indulged, spoiled children, this all-too-common syndrome is profoundly and completely preventable.

Can You Hear Me Now?

I once did a series of local TV news appearances where we would show video clips of "behavior makeovers," and then open the lines for viewers to phone in with questions. A caller complained that her cute little bichon crossbreed had developed an embarrassing habit. Whenever they were out in public and the owner took attention away from her dog, it would bark and scream wildly at the top of its lungs. Its nonstop yapping was so high pitched and piercing, it was impossible for the woman to carry on any kind of conversation or consumer transaction.

The owner added that she had worked with four separate trainers to the tune of $2,000—all to no avail. In a tone that lacked conviction, the woman asked if I could help. I looked right into the camera and asked her to call me after the show, assuring her that I would fix the problem.

I was fully confident I could calm this vociferous dog in very short order. After we talked, I invited the lady to the TV studio where we filmed a brief interview. I had asked the woman to tie her dog outside the building near the main entrance, explaining that we would conduct our interview in the lobby. We were close enough to monitor her dog's tantrum, yet far enough away that we could hear each other. Throughout the interview, the dog (which we could see through the glass-encased foyer) screamed wildly in the background. There was plenty of good footage showing the dog as it freaked out.

The woman and I then took her little fiend for a walk. First, I showed the owner how to use the training collar and line, and every time her dog interrupted a social interlude with barks, the woman made a quick correction. The little dog soon got the message. Just one hour later, we returned with a completely calm and quiet pooch. Again, we tied the dog outside and went inside the building. The lady was amazed to see her dog remain still and silent. In our interview, I asked for her reactions to the dog's "new" behavior. The owner was astounded that such a result could be achieved so quickly and easily. When the "before and after" footage was aired, my phone was busy for quite some time!

Desperate Measures

It should come as no surprise that an effective training regimen of praise plus fair, firm, and consistent discipline is the only long-term answer to separation anxiety issues. But too many owners, influenced by the language and labels that excuse problematic pet behaviors, fall into the trap of treating the symptoms instead of addressing the cause. I'm perplexed and saddened at the numbers of people who turn to alternative "solutions." My biggest bugaboo is drugs.

The distraught owners of dogs that chronically misbehave often beg, plead, and pressure their veterinarians to "Please do something." The vets, busy and ill equipped to provide practical training advice, resort to their one available option for calming the animals—chemicals. Despite the potentially harmful side effects of drugs, frantic owners place blind trust in the professionals, not realizing they are only masking the problem with medication, not making it go away.

There's an even more desperate measure that has recently come on the scene: the surgical removal of an incessant barker's larynx, or voice box. To their credit, most veterinarians caution dog owners that "surgical bark removal" (as it is called) should be used only as a last resort. I contend that it should not be a consideration at all. Owners that have reached their wit's end opt for this drastic procedure because today's popular positive reinforcement training methods aren't working. The training is failing the dog, so owners feel forced to take desperate measures to make the problem disappear. Regrettably, this inhumane surgery only produces the *illusion* of a solution. The dog's mental state remains the same while the owners delude themselves into thinking the problem has been fixed.

Rescue Dog

And now we cover our last social label that can too often cause long-term distress for both dogs and owners. We are all familiar with the term "rescue dog." This is another phrase worth analyzing because you can probably infer that the word itself, *rescue*, can erode an owner's resolve to properly correct behavioral issues as they surface. Granted, many rescue dogs are indeed liberated from horrific circumstances, the extremes of which are almost unfathomable.

It is sickening and distressing to consider the degree of abuse and evil that happens to animals in every culture, and it goes without saying that such maltreatment leaves not only physical, but mental, scars. Given that reality, should anyone choose to take on the awesome responsibility of adopting a formerly abused rescue dog, they must be acutely aware of their perceptions and actions so they don't enable or perpetuate their pet's behavior problems.

When people generously open their hearts and homes to a rescue dog, they want to do everything possible to provide a safe, nurturing shelter for their adoptee. It's a huge gesture, an honorable intention, a lot of work, and a colossal commitment, to be sure. You can imagine the heartwarming satisfaction those owners feel when their dogs look up at them with love-filled eyes as if to say, "Thank you for saving me. You are wonderful for giving me such a good life." It's a beautiful testament to the kindness of the human heart. But some well-intentioned owners go too far; they fall into a "kindness" trap that threatens to undo all of the goodness attached to their generosity. These owners continually try to make up for their rescue dog's painful past with spoiling, permissiveness, and justification for bad behavior.

Consider for a moment that if a rescue dog were adopted by a pack of canines instead of human beings, his four-legged family would not know his history. Members of the pack would not grant any partiality or leniency to compensate for what the rescue dog had been forced to endure in the past. The new dog would simply have to carry on with its life and adapt to its new, better circumstances: a safe existence with fair, firm, and consistent discipline to maintain order and harmony. A life where affection, acceptance, and the freedom to operate within established boundaries would be the norm.

The rescue dog would have to deal with an initiation period that may involve corrections from the pack leader for certain "social offenses," to help the adoptee to properly settle in. In other words, the new pack member would be subjected to measures of discipline and correction, imposed without guilt or apology. After finding his place within the hierarchy, the new dog would be free to relax and play and enjoy life with his newfound companions. Once he learned and adapted to the clearly delineated social rules, the dog could look forward to a joyful, peaceful life.

A Win-Win Situation

We do our dogs no favors when we treat them like little furry, four-footed human beings. We shortchange them when we take on the role of perpetual rescuer. This parallels the lesson that parents of disabled children have to learn: firm, fair, and consistent discipline is an expression of love. And not exercising these essential life-shaping skills can have grave unintended consequences.

All of my dogs have been rescue dogs. I'm not suggesting that, as owners of rescue dogs, we should lay all emotions aside and take a coldhearted militaristic approach to training. I'm saying it's critical that we realize and accept the fact that everything we *can* do for our dogs is not necessarily best for our dogs. Here's what I mean: while we *can* impose our human values on our dogs and excuse, allow, and tolerate misconduct, everyone loses out in the end. It makes more sense that we'd want to go for a win-win instead. It may seem odd that we as pet owners are in our most wise and powerful state when we let go of our humanistic labels and "think like a dog." But given the wealth of examples in this book, what other conclusion could we draw?

CHAPTER 14

No alibi will save you from accepting the responsibility. —Napoleon Hill

RUBES®   **By Leigh Rubin**

Obedience Means Never Having to Make Excuses

WHILE FILMING MY first infomercial, my wife and I took our boys and dog to a village on the California coast that featured an off-leash dog park right on the beach. Judah, our German shorthaired pointer, had an absolute ball, blissfully threading his way through the crowds of people and dogs, connecting with every creature willing to befriend him. I had a hi-def video camera with me to capture some B-roll for the show.

We delighted in watching Judah's exhilaration as he bounded across the sand, exploring, interacting, and relishing his freedom—all the while behaving like a perfect gentleman. Getting to watch our dog in a state of unfettered bliss was our reward for all the training time we'd invested. These memorable moments fuel our passion to continue our work of empowering other dog owners with the knowledge and skills necessary to create nonaggressive, mature, and trustworthy off-leash companions.

However, our pleasure dwindled as we took a second look at our surroundings and let the scene before us truly register. Not everyone was having such an idyllic experience. We noted numerous apprehensive owners with leashed dogs held tightly in their grasp. Their closely monitored pets straining at the ends of their short tethers bore an unhappy resemblance to prisoners, with eyes cast longingly at their peers freely galloping and gamboling in the sand.

Our hearts went out to these poor animals, sentenced to a day of mental torture as they stood so near, yet so far from freedom. We knew that this sad scene represented a snapshot of the overall quality of life these dogs lived every day. In all likelihood, these pathetic pooches had in some way proven themselves to be unreliable to a degree, but they weren't the real culprits. Some might say the blame lay solely in the hands of the owners, but we knew there was more going on than met the eye. In truth, these constricted canines and their owners were the unwitting victims of a nearsighted culture that perpetuates a warped and sadly limited vision of dogs and their true training potential.

Running Aground

Off in one direction, we saw three leashed dachshunds swirling around their owner's ankles as he made futile attempts to untangle the mess. While the owner preoccupied himself with the snarled strips of cord, one of his little dainties aggressively hurled herself toward a dog that managed to remain free from her advance. The dachshund's launch was brought to an abrupt and startling halt as she hit the end of her restraint. After her spill, she righted herself, slightly stunned but still with her dander up, surveying the surroundings for her next unsuspecting prey.

Elsewhere, a Boston terrier was briefly engaged in momentary romps with other pups, only to be quickly abandoned by his playmates as they wandered beyond the confines of the terrier's rope. You could almost feel his heart sink as each potential playmate disappeared. Yet with evident hope, he waited for the next turn of this cruel carousel, despite his mounting disappointment with each pass.

Everywhere we looked, there was a different experience going on, a different story line. Perhaps we were projecting, but some of the leash-bearing owners seemed wistful or possibly even envious as they observed Judah and the other well-mannered dogs freely romping about. With absorbed expressions, they seemed to be pondering the contrast—as if to wonder what it might take to enjoy such liberties in a public place.

Hit the Beach

And then we saw it, a drove of freewheeling dogs running full tilt and out of control, far ahead of their clueless owners. Having seen this kind of madness before, we've named it Club Chaos—owner and dog duos that give off-leash freedom a very bad rap. As a consequence, our mood went from sad to sour, knowing that a good deal of negative energy was about to be unleashed on our once-tranquil setting.

These rogue dogs held no regard for anyone or anything in their path as they plundered, pillaged, and promulgated disruption with their wild, riotous behavior. As the canine tornado touched down, unsuspecting spectators and bystanders were struck, slammed, and plowed into. The dogs wrestled, ran, and wrangled with each other, spreading their havoc far and wide. Blankets were soiled. Belongings were scattered. Towels were ground into the sand by big dog feet. The hurricane of canines also left their "territorial markings" on assorted coolers, backpacks, and other personal items as the dogs blew through the densely populated beach. Meanwhile, the owners of these beasts were barely in sight, which was hardly a surprise. It was quite a scene.

From our vantage point, we felt like movie extras in a scene from the canine version of *Beach Blanket Bingo*. Fortunately, we hadn't been in the direct path of Club Chaos, but a lot of adults and kids had been momentarily disrupted by their wake. This experience was so far removed from our own family's everyday life with Judah that our jaws were practically on our chests. We wondered if anyone else was equally flabbergasted, or if the locals considered it just another day at the dog beach.

It Doesn't Have To Be This Way

Whenever I witness dysfunction like this, I dream of standing in front of a crowd with a large megaphone in hand, declaring to one and all, "It doesn't have to be this way!" Truly, it was within the grasp of *every* dog owner present that day to enjoy a perfect time at the beach, yet their knowledge and skills fell short of the mark. Whether they knew it or not, many of these dog owners desperately needed someone to offer insight, guidance, and technique.

We all know there's a difference between wanting something and getting it. Wishing is not enough. The secret is in educating ourselves and then taking action on our newfound knowledge. Too many people choose to remain clueless about what it means to be one of those "responsible dog owners," and we all suffer from their ignorance.

Experience tells me that the majority of people who most needed counsel that day would have become defensive had I approached them. I would have heard the same excuses and justifications I'm always given. "Oh, my dog is just distracted because it's so busy here." "He's still only a puppy." "He didn't start the fight." Or, "We *are* going to training and he's coming along nicely." Even if I had countered these arguments with concrete suggestions, these people—like so many others—would have insisted that their dogs were good dogs. But of course, this begs the question of what the word "good" really means in terms of behavior and the standards by which progress is measured.

If you ever find yourself saying something like "My dog is really well behaved, except for . . ." then take particular notice of what follows this phrase. Whenever I'm faced with this oft-repeated preamble, I'm tempted to translate the statement into what it really means. In reality, the sentence should go like this: "My dog only listens half the time and he has some behavioral issues, but I allow my love and devotion to cloud my vision so that I overlook and make excuses for his faults." *There is a vast difference between loving your dog while tolerating his faults, and truly enjoying your dog because his presence enriches your life in a multitude of ways.*

Dogs live an average of thirteen years of age, and each pet's life span represents a fairly significant portion of our own lives on this earth. The *quality* of the years we will spend with our dogs is entirely up to us. If we submit to the pressure of societal myths and self-deception, we will likely resign ourselves to life with a self-absorbed, troublesome canine that develops into more of a liability than a true companion. But we can instead fully realize the hopes, dreams, and goals we held in our hearts the day we brought our dog home, using my tools and techniques to build a mutually fulfilling relationship.

The Way It Can Be

By now you have a sense of how much I respect the canine species. I love dogs—I always have. I love them enough to have dedicated a large part of my life and livelihood toward creating a better world for family pets. In working with my own dogs, I've discovered how rewarding and wonderful a well-trained dog can be, and sometimes seeing them in action brings tears to my eyes. I wish I could instantly transfer my knowledge and experience to other owners, but they would need to be open, curious, and willing to change.

Things can be different. The lives of all dogs can be improved and enhanced once their owners open their minds and awaken to all the possibilities that exist. If this sounds dramatic, that is my intention; perhaps it helps you grasp the depth of my conviction. People *can* free themselves from the binding mind-set of pitifully low standards set by prevalent social myths and the pressure of false expectation. Why should anyone settle for less than they deserve in the relationships they share with their pets? After all, our dogs are a part of the family.

As citizens of this world, we are accountable for how we live our lives. Our animals are an extension of our standards, beliefs, values, and lifestyle. Instead of caving in and staying our course on the path of least resistance, we need to be autonomous and reject popular trends that make absolutely no sense. We need to practice self-discipline by refusing to superimpose human characteristics on our animals. By respecting the dog's instincts and experiences, we can connect with the inner wisdom of the canine spirit and practice a manner of discipline our dogs can understand.

And last, when we have put forth consistent effort in creating a perfect dog, the consequences we live with will be respect, trust, safety, freedom, and fun instead of misbehavior, recrimination, incarceration, and possible costs we could never conjure in our wildest dreams. In comparing these highly contrasting outcomes, how could anyone consider the latter for even a fleeting moment?

It's in Your Hands

Your dog didn't get to choose who his owner would be. *You* were privileged with that choice. Therefore, you owe it to your beloved pet to provide him with the best life possible. A good dog is an obedient dog, and true obedience means never having to excuse or justify your dog's behavior. You and your pet deserve all this and more. A whole new way of living awaits you and your beloved dog. Are you willing to do what it takes to make it happen? If so, don't hesitate. Don't wait. Start now and don't stop. A whole new future is within your grasp, and it's yours for the taking.

Rubes® — By Leigh Rubin

A Real-Life "Lassie" Moment

RETURNING FROM A camping trip with my dog Wise, I pulled up our sloped driveway and parked my truck. The small utility trailer was still attached to the bumper hitch, heavily loaded down with camping gear. I absentmindedly unhooked the trailer so I could roll it into its usual spot where it would sit until my next trip. Tired, preoccupied, and happy to be home, I had never attempted this maneuver with a fully loaded trailer before.

The moment I detached the trailer, I realized that I was in trouble. Between the weight of the trailer and degree of the slope, physical forces beyond my limits were taking over. Basically, the trailer was poised to roll down the driveway and into the street. With all my might, I fought to keep the trailer from rolling down the slope. Talk about a stalemate! I could stop the trailer from rolling any farther, but I was powerless to either reattach it to the truck or steer it to any safe location.

I called out in desperation for anyone within earshot to come help, but I was on my own. Looking around for anyone or anything that might get me out of this jam, I saw Wise lying in the yard enjoying the fresh air after our long drive home. I called her name, and as she neared me, I moved my head in a circular fashion, pointing with my eyes to a large piece of firewood lying on the side of the driveway. I asked her to pick up the firewood and bring it to me. Keep in mind that both of my hands were braced against the trailer, so hand signals were impossible. All of my communication with Wise happened with my words and the careful motioning of my head.

Following my commands in perfect order, Wise grabbed onto the oversized piece of wood and began dragging it in my direction. Before she reached me, I asked that she alter her course slightly and move past me, so she would end up next to the nearest trailer wheel. I then instructed her to drop the wood, which she did immediately.

My dog's flawless execution of this delicate task enabled me to gingerly release my hold on the trailer. Just as I'd hoped, the trailer pivoted slightly and slipped into place as its weight settled in, now safely braced against the block.

My dog and friend, Wise, had come to my aid and rescued me from what otherwise could have been an ugly accident, endangering not just me, but perhaps any passersby. My dog's ability to read my unusual signals when life and limb were in jeopardy was truly a touching testimony to the unity and mutual understanding we shared.

This was just one of my many "Lassie" moments with Wise, demonstrating that dogs trained to a level of self-governance are capable of far more than we might think. These are the kinds of memories that stay with me forever and encourage me to fervently and passionately continue my rewarding work.

MORE PRAISE FOR THE DOGFATHER'S *PERFECT DOG®* SYSTEM

As I worked as a positive reinforcement trainer, I found myself disagreeing with some of the things I was told, such as "Your dog doesn't remember" or "Just ignore the behavior." When I found your system (which I sought out after adopting a puppy that tested me in every way possible), my life totally changed. You were saying everything I'd been looking for. Your system totally transformed both of my dogs—even my Lab that I thought was very well trained. But now, wow! She is perfect!

It'll be so nice now that I'm expecting my first child, to be able to walk my Lab off leash next to the stroller. And my small dog that was such a nightmare at first is now a blessing and a joy to have in my life. I've gone back to training dogs the way I used to before the "no correction" positive reinforcement kick started, proudly showing off my dogs as proof of how well your system works. Thank you for bringing this type of training back. I recommend your system to anyone who asks about the best way to train a dog.
Maggie S.

Our dog Barkley was a terror: he chewed, he barked, he ran around our house like he was on fire. When he chewed the spindles on our staircase, my husband told me that I had to do something or Barkley was headed out the door. I was in tears. On the one hand, this dog was the most loving, sweet little guy when he wanted to be but on the other hand, my husband and I couldn't bear to watch this crazy little dog tear our house apart!

I saw the infomercial for your training a few weeks ago, and considered it because of Barkley's mischievous ways. After a conversation with my husband, I purchased your system, which I received four days ago. The first thing I noticed was how much information your DVDs cover! As recommended, I watched the initial training segments on DVD number 1, and then I set out on a walk to work on leash pulling. I was AMAZED that,

125

in literally five minutes, my dog was walking with me without pulling! Even more amazing was the fact that when I would stop walking, he would also stop AND LIE DOWN! I couldn't believe it.

In four days, Barkley has learned to walk without pulling on his leash, he has learned "down," "down and stay" (even when I throw his toy in front of him!), "retrieve," and "come." My husband can't believe it. Your philosophy on training is something I hadn't heard before (most of the time, you hear about training with treat rewards), but when I listen to you speak about the mind-set of dogs, it makes so much sense.

To see the change in my dog in just four days is unbelievable. I can't wait to see what we can accomplish in the next four days! If I had to pick my favorite part of this training so far, it was seeing the happiness on Barkley's face last night as he got to play "retrieve" with me for the first time ever, outside where he could run freely.

I would recommend these DVDs to anyone and everyone with a dog. If my little terror can change so much in a matter of minutes, it can work for anyone! Thank you, Thank you!

Jennifer W.

I breed Labrador retrievers and have tried in the past to obedience train my dogs based on my twenty-five years of experience as a breeder. I recently ordered your program along with a few additional Command Collars so I could start working with my older dogs and my young pups. I have noticed *immediate* results. In fact, I was shocked at how fast my dogs responded. I can't express how wonderful it is to be able to trust my dogs and to actually enjoy working with them. It's no longer a chore; it's fun!

One of the main reasons I ordered your program is that my twenty-four-year-old daughter has Usher's syndrome; she's profoundly deaf and slowly losing her eyesight. My goal is to teach her nine-month-old pup to assist her in the future. I've only been using your system for approximately three weeks, and the pup is doing great! She completely focuses on my daughter, responds to sign language, and is learning something new every day. I cannot find the words to express the feeling I get seeing my daughter interact with her new companion.

I've been working with dogs for over two decades, and I thought I knew how to "basic obedience train" my dogs. *I honestly have learned more in the past three to four weeks than I ever have.* I sincerely appreciate what you have done with your system and the "gift" you have given us through your wisdom. I know my dogs appreciate it too!

I encourage everyone that adopts a pup from me to purchase your program; that way, I know my pups and their owners will enjoy their lives together. Thank you again from one extremely satisfied customer!

Michelle K. Bloomington, IL.

This is the best investment I've ever made! I was a little skeptical at first, but we were desperate to correct our dog's bad habits, so I ordered your system. And I'm glad I did! It does work as advertised; I have seen results in a matter of minutes!

I've had remarkable results training my Jack Russell mix, Pacsi. We got her as a stray. She had been used to surviving on the streets alone, so she had more than a few bad habits such as running off on her own and knocking over trash cans to scrounge for food. A couple of times, she came home with what had to have been someone's lunch!

We used to have a problem with Pacsi bolting out the front door, but after only a few weeks of us using your *Perfect Dog®* program, she is like a different dog! Now when I open the front door, she will not cross the threshold unless I call her out. And when we go for walks, she stays right there with me! We're at the point where I can walk her using the three-foot Freedom Line, and I don't even have to hold on to it. Hopefully soon, we'll be at the point where we can walk leash free!

For anyone who thinks this system is cruel to the dog, let me tell you it's not! Pacsi still showers us with affection and vice-versa. Our friends and relatives have seen the change themselves, and now they are going to try it with their dogs.

Scott H. Texas, USA.

The fact that your training DVDs have been so masterfully structured and concisely edited, and the fact that your instructions simply leave no doubt as to what is correct and what won't work, has resulted in what I would consider the best-trained, freest dog I've ever been around! And that's just in the first six months of her life, and just the first six weeks since I bought your program. After I watched the DVDs, I thought, "Wow! I can't think of a single thing he left out. This guy has done a GREAT job of putting things together! It's all there."

I spoke today with a friend of mine at work who has owned Labradors for years. I told her that my six-month-old dog could now do commands with incredible reliability. She can "sit," "down," "stay," "wait," "come," "sit" at a distance, "go pee," and "go to the bathroom." And she does more, such as "play" (which tells her she has the freedom to play) and "that's far enough" (which keeps her from wandering beyond an acceptable distance). After owning dogs for years, my friend was amazed at all my puppy can do, and so quickly! She said to me, "You sure have a smart dog." I told her it's not the dog; it's Don Sullivan's training.

Around the office, we're all into photography, and we have some of the world's leading photographers on our staff. We all know a story about being at dinner and showing photos to others at the table when the waitress commented, "Those are great pictures! You must have a great camera." When the check came, the photographer said to the waitress, "That was an excellent meal! You must have great pots." I think that really kind of covers it. Sure, I have a great dog, but it's mostly because of a great training system!   *Larry B. Tampa, Florida.*

You have given us back our life! I wish we had your training program months ago! We got an Old English sheepdog pup from a breeder who had the pup returned at eleven weeks old because the owners could not control her. She was fine when we picked her up, but after two days, all hell broke loose. She was aggressive, arrogant, and way out of control. My hands and arms were so sore from the biting and scratching. Even though I could have cried, I wasn't going to because that would have meant she had won.

We went to dog training classes, but after ten months, the improvement was very slight. It was exhausting because she would not listen (in the classes they used the "talk-to-the-hand" method, and it wasn't working). Several times we thought about giving her up, but we knew she would probably end up in a rescue for the rest of her life.

Your Command Collar® has given us a voice that she can't ignore, and she has improved greatly. We are now getting compliments on having such a well-trained dog.   *Sarah. Reading, Berkshire, Great Britain.*

Just a week before I saw your infomercial, I was thinking of finding a new home for my dog. But now I'm on day three, and it's like I have a new dog—a good dog! I would recommend your system to anyone who is having troubles with their dog. It works! Your methods make more sense than anything else I've tried.

I had been trying various training plans with no success. Rose (my dog, a Thailand Ridgeback) is not interested in treats for the most part, so clicker training and such methods were useless with her. I have more collars than I can count: no pull, choke, halti, no-pull harnesses. Nothing worked. I have several clickers and books on training, including some from famous TV trainers. Nothing helped: she pulled, pulled, pulled.

My daughter, who has done a lot of research on dog training for her dog, recommended your *Perfect Dog*® DVDs. This was after we left the dog to board for a few days at a veterinarian's office and she attacked the staff. I was concerned she would bite someone and that I would lose her.

The DVDs are fabulous. The advice is so practical and effective. Our first walk was a learning period for both of us. By the second walk, I had learned how to correct, and the difference is amazing. No more sore shoulders and arms, and no more being dragged across the street. We now enjoy our walks together.

I have Rose wear the Command Collar® and the shorter Freedom Training Line in the house, and the difference is amazing: she seems calmer already. We're going to start "down" and "stay" in the next few days. I'm truly looking forward to the day when Rose can walk off leash and we can be happy together as it should be with dog and owner, and I don't think that's too far away.   *Charla Van V. Los Angeles, California.*

I want to say that your training program is EXCELLENT! I have a six-year-old German shepherd that has been running our household since she was a puppy. We were aggravated, tired, and at our wits end with her, and then I saw your infomercial for the *Perfect Dog*® product. I thought, "Well, I don't have anything to lose," and I decided to try the program. Unbelievably, I saw positive results the day I started training!

My husband thought I was a kook for buying these DVDs, and he thought it would never work on our dog. Well, he was really surprised, and then he started watching the DVDs too. We're about four days into our training, and already, there has been a dramatic change in her attitude.

I look forward to continuing her training and seeing the full results. I would recommend your program to ANYONE with an out-of-control dog. Thank you, Don, for putting these DVDs out there.   *Nicole H.*

I bought your *Secrets to Training the Perfect Dog* ® program, and it has worked better than anything I've ever tried. I have an eight-month-old Lab/German shepherd mix. He would constantly run toward other dogs every time we turned our backs. Also, every time we played fetch with him, he would run off with his toy, and it would be gone forever. When he ran off and I tried to call him back, he would not even think about obeying. Now, every time I call him, even if he's playing with other dogs, he returns to me.

I tried treat training, but my dog would not listen to me if he knew I didn't have a treat in my hand, and it took a month to teach him "sit." But even when I had treats, he would constantly run off. After a few weeks of using your methods in only fifteen minutes a day during the week and a little more on the weekends, I have taught him "sit," "down," and "stay" (which is really impressive and very useful). And I can work outside and around the house for twelve to fourteen hours, and he will never leave our front yard.

It's such a relief to not have to chase our dog and worry about him all the time. I cannot wait to continue your system. He is really the dog I always wanted right now, and I can't imagine the improvements to come in a few more weeks.   *Jeremy. Blacksburg, South Carolina.*

I love your system. It is well prepared and thought out, and highly effective. I am so impressed with it that I'm planning to incorporate it into the animal shelter where I volunteer in the Northwest Territories, Canada. We get many large dogs—huskies, pit bulls, shepherds—and many very small-breed dogs. Most are abused and abandoned. Many have been raised in "puppy mill" type homes. I would like to start training them in the basics with your system and put them in better homes. I would also like to start training some of them with your advanced methods so they can be given as companion animals and, eventually, working dogs.

I found your DVDs to be very well prepared and explained. And I like your loving approach. I'm teaching my children with your DVDs as well. Your information not only helps with our dogs, but with life in general. I'm hoping to start a prison dog training program with your methods to help inmates (most often abused and abandoned) take control of their lives and learn forgiveness, patience, and compassion.

Robyn H. Fort Smith, Canada.

I have a Pomeranian puppy, Luci. We started out OK. When I brought her home, she dealt with the crate wonderfully, but all hell was about to break loose. She pee-peed where she wanted and refused to do poo outside. She chewed up everything she could reach: shoes, mail, rubber tips on doorstops, glasses, pens, you name it. Nothing was safe. No matter how hard I baby proofed, she found a way to get around it. She barked so shrill that it shivered your bones; she tormented the cats, pulled on the leash, tripped me, and had separation anxiety like you wouldn't believe. She whined, cried, jumped, licked, nipped, and chewed my hands. If you can name it, she did it.

I read, searched the Internet, tried the Dog Whisperer tips, and received advice from friends. I cried, screamed, and I was humiliated with her chewing up houseguests' personal items. I had reached the decision that Luci needed to go to a new home. I was flipping channels and your *Perfect Dog®* infomercial popped up. I watched you change dogs in minutes. Truthfully, I figured it was another trip down Rip-off Drive. I looked at Luci and said, "Okay, one more try," and I even did the $10 "get it to me now" option!

Luci took to the collar immediately. wow, who is this new dog? She has taken on a whole new body language. I'm no longer frustrated and shaking. She's listening and cooperating. I called my ex-husband and told him about the new program. We actually got to talk on the phone without her barking, biting, licking, and jumping all over me.

WONDERFUL, FABULOUS, OUTSTANDING. This is unbelievable! We now take walks around the property without the tug-of-war barking battle. Don Sullivan, you have saved my dog from being evicted from my home. I know the rest of the training will go well. I have the companion I hoped for when I brought her home. I just needed to be trained on how to train her. I'd love to be able to thank you in person. I will recommend your system to everyone. I'm sure that Luci thanks you too.

Kathy

INDEX

133

Humane Society, 107, 134